TSUNAMI KIDS

THE GANDY BROTHERS

With Nick Harding

Michael O'Mara Books Limited

Dedicated to Mum and Dad and all those
affected by the events of 26 December 2004

Contents

Maelstrom

I FELT IT BEFORE it hit. The world shook in the seconds before it bore down on us with the full force of nature. It sucked the humid tropical air away, replacing it with a solid wall of angry water, thick with mud and debris. In an instant everything became noise, energy and panic.

It came surging through the front of the building in a roaring torrent, sweeping trees, buildings and vehicles away; swatting them like flies.

I heard the distant rumble first and saw fear on the faces of the few people dotted around the hotel complex before it reached us. They'd seen it approach from the horizon. Instinct kicked in. A fight or flight adrenaline surge shocked me into action and I ran back into the room where my brother Paul was starting to rouse from sleep.

I screamed at him. Something was coming. The roar got louder. It crashed ashore with megaton energy. There was no chance to think. Reaction. Survival. We were just a few yards back from the beach and in its path. It would have hit the villa my parents and younger siblings were in first then, milliseconds later, it was upon us.

I spun round as the water engulfed our room, which was a flimsy house of cards against the deluge. It crashed against the front wall and was suddenly everywhere at once and rising in a torrent. The door was ripped from its hinges as it gushed in. The windows gave way immediately. Shards of glass flew towards us like bullets. I raised my arms to protect my face and felt a momentary burning pain across the underside of my upper arm.

The water was dark and brown. The noise was deafening. I shouted to Paul again. We needed to get out. The room was filling up with sea water; a briny coffin. I thought the island was sinking. Outside, the sea had replaced the land. It was the end of the world. I couldn't compute what was happening. All I could do was react. All around us the furniture was being picked up and smashed apart as if made of matchsticks. The sink was ripped off the wall and shattered into ceramic daggers.

I knew we both needed to stay on our feet or the current swirling around us would sweep us off our legs and wash us away. I felt debris smash against my shins. It took just seconds for the water to reach thigh height. It was rushing past the door, heading inland at what seemed like hundreds of miles an hour.

'Get out!' I yelled to Paul. He was on his feet, trying to walk towards me. I twisted round, grabbed his hand and pulled him towards me as I steadied myself against the battering currents. I took a shaky stride forward towards the doorway, straining against the force of the surge that was gushing through it. The water was now waist-high and continuing to rise. Outside I glimpsed branches, sunbeds and whole trees being carried past on the tide. The thunderous roar continued to fill my head.

I inched forward and managed to get out through the door. I grabbed the door frame and pulled myself out of the room. With the other hand I helped Paul step free of the building.

A brick wall ran across the veranda at the front of the villa and, using a pole that supported the roof, I pulled myself onto it and grabbed another pole that ran across the lip of the roof. I tried to pull Paul up next to me as the current attemped to drag him away.

I held onto Paul's hand with grim determination. The wall underneath me gave way beneath my feet, washed away as if it was made of sand. I hung there, suspended. One hand gripped the metal bar, the other gripped my brother. If I let go of Paul, he would be washed away to certain death. If I let go of the bar, we'd both be killed.

All around us was chaos. The world was being washed away. Buildings were collapsing in on themselves, flimsy under the weight of the sea. Roofs were ripped off and crumbled to pieces, absorbed by the thick, chocolate-coloured water. Uprooted trees smashed into a soup of floating wreckage. Nearby power lines came down and hung menacingly in the water, sparking as they hit the flow.

To this day, I have no idea where the strength came from. I was a scrawny seventeen-year-old and Paul was only slightly smaller than me and two years younger. But, somehow, I managed to pull us both high enough out of the water for Paul to grab the bar too. Perhaps, in a bitter irony, the waters that were threatening to kill us both rose high enough to give us an extra bit of buoyancy.

We clung to the edge of the roof and pulled ourselves free of the rising wave.

'Higher,' I called to my brother and we both scrambled further up the roof as the lowest row of tiles was swept away. We climbed to the apex, the very highest point we could reach. We were both barefoot and the rough terracotta grated on the soles of our feet. We felt no pain. We were numb and breathless.

And then it started to wane. The torrent started to slow. It did not rise any higher and its destructive journey inland became gentler. Eddies swirled debris in lazy circles. In the distance I heard the clanging and scraping. The wave ebbed.

For the first time, I had a chance to look around properly. The world had ended. Everywhere was submerged. I couldn't see a soul. It was Boxing Day 2004. The previous night we'd celebrated Christmas in the open-air restaurant. It had been strung with fairy lights and the waiters had worn Santa hats. We'd played games and surfed in the day. Now everything was destroyed.

And then I wondered where our parents were.

CHAPTER 1

The Purley King and Queen

EVERY JOURNEY STARTS with a footstep; a single stride forward. Motion and direction. Our journey starts with Kevin Forkan, a man who always grabbed life with both hands and squeezed it until the pips fell out. Kevin was an adventurer, a visionary and a thoroughly decent bloke who lived by his wits and guile and always did what he believed was right. He travelled the world and along the way he got into a few scrapes. It built his character. In business he was fearless and forward-thinking. Kevin loved life, he loved people and he valued experience and family. He'd hitch-hiked across South Africa and lived in America and Australia before he settled down to run his own car showroom which was located in a place called Mitcham, the car-dealer capital of south London.

In the early eighties, when Kevin set up his showroom, Mitcham was full of men in sheepskin coats with questionable moral compasses, lured there by Mitcham Car Auctions, a sprawling conveyor belt where vehicles changed hands and the phrase 'sold as seen' was used regularly as a form of magical incantation with the power to protect against grievances relating to mileage and MOT provenance. Kevin wasn't like his peers, however. In the world of car salesmen, he was an anomaly. He was a bit of a geezer but a decent bloke, and I never saw him wear a sheepskin coat.

To us, Kevin was simply 'Dad'. A larger-than-life, unique, free-spirited, driven man with a great *joie de vivre*, which is probably why Mum fell for him despite the fourteen-year age gap.

Dad was the reason we saw the world. He was infected with the travel bug and he passed that on to us. He'd been given his itchy feet by his own family. Some of them came from Ireland and the Irish blood coursing through his veins was probably the reason he went off on his travels at a young age. Before he set up his business, he travelled all over the world. He told us the stories. He recalled being in Mexico in the seventies where, when he crossed the border into America, he was held at gunpoint by US police who suspected he was a drug-runner. He described the hustle and bustle of New York and he waxed lyrical about Australia. It was the days before widely available cheap air fares so he mainly travelled by boat. It was all good dinnertime conversation.

Dad was the youngest of five, with three brothers and a sister. His brother John was another avid adventurer who had travelled extensively through Europe and Asia, crossing Afghanistan and Pakistan before settling down in Australia with his wife, Anne.

Dad would crack out his travel stories after a beer or two. Mum would raise her eyebrows. One of his favourite yarns involved a Porsche sports car, Miss Australia, a ravine and a near miss.

Before he met Mum, he had been in Australia visiting John and been to a party where he happened to meet Miss Australia. Dad was driving a 911 coupé at the time. He'd bought it while he was there and asked John to find him a personal plate for it. John duly obliged with an act of brotherly jocularity and Dad ended up driving the flash car with the word 'PU55Y' displayed front and back. Nevertheless, when Dad offered Miss Australia a lift home she accepted. None of us know whether Dad was showing off at the time but, on the way, he lost control of the powerful car, spun off a bridge and careered down a ravine. The car was totalled but Dad and Miss Australia miraculously walked away without serious injury.

Dad's early wanderings were curtailed when he set up his own business. His other UK-based brothers also owned car showrooms so it seemed a natural choice of business. He was a hard worker and did well in the car trade. No doubt his expanded world view set him apart from some of the other Arthur Daley-type characters who operated in the trade at the time.

Dad was a keen sportsman and very active. He played cricket, tennis and football and he enjoyed watching sports as well as playing them. He was an avid Queen's Park Rangers fan which, over the years and to coin a phrase, taught him how to meet triumph and disaster and treat those two impostors the same.

He was tall and athletic with dark hair; all in all a decent-looking bloke.

His life changed for ever the day he employed our mum, Sandra, as his assistant. Young, tall and tanned with flowing curls, it was one of her first jobs and she was taken on to do reception and admin duties.

Romance blossomed in the Ford franchise and, eventually, Kevin and Sandra married and set about finding a family home.

Initially they looked at houses in Fulham and Chelsea; now extremely affluent areas of south-west London full of oligarchs and foreign investors. But back then, properties in those parts of the capital, while expensive, were not subject to the same multi-million-pound price tags they command today. There were still bargains to be had and Dad had always been good at spotting an opportunity.

However, Mum and Dad wanted a big family and for that they needed space. So eventually they decided that the hustle and bustle of London might not be the best place to raise young children. In London they also discovered that they didn't get much garden for their budget, and one of their house-hunting prerequisites was to end up in a place with a garden large enough for their brood to run around in. Eventually they settled in Purley, a leafy London district a few miles from the town of Croydon, in a road called Meadow Close. There was no meadow in it, but it sounded nice. It was close enough to make the commute to Dad's showroom comfortable, but far enough away from the town to afford a bit of space, peace and greenery. Together they chose a house which, while it wasn't a mansion, was homely and big enough for a sizeable family. It had a small front drive with enough room for one car and the advantage of a big rear garden. They set about making it into a home. Any further ambitions Dad had to travel were put aside. In fact, you wouldn't have known that he had travelled. He didn't have any souvenirs around the house; instead it was a typical family home with family pictures on the mantelpiece above the open fire in the lounge.

They did up the inside of the house but they weren't gardeners which, in the long run, was just as well. Mum sometimes tried to potter around in the garden. Occasionally she'd buy some shrubs or flowers but the procession of young children they had over the following years put paid to any green-fingered ambitions. No sooner was a flower planted than it was destroyed by hands, feet, balls, bats or racquets. The garden remained much as it was when they bought it: laid to lawn with some big trees in it – an open space.

In 1983, the Forkan family got its first addition. Mum had my eldest sister, Marie. In 1985, Joanne – Jo – came along. Two years later, I was born. I was christened Robert Oliver Daniel Forkan. The names were chosen specifically because my initials were an anagram of FORD, like my dad's showroom. Clearly he was a bit of a joker – I'm just thankful he didn't have an Alfa Romeo franchise!

My brothers Paul and Matthew – or Mattie – were born in 1989 and 1992 respectively and finally Rosie, our little sister, came along. She was the princess of the family, the final one. The eight of us all lived in homely chaos with Mum and Dad at the helm.

Although the house was spacious, we still had to share rooms at one time or another because there were so many of us. I shared a room with Paul for most of my childhood and when they were little, Mattie and Rosie shared too.

We messed around, we fought but generally we all got on well. We were a pack and in any pack there is a hierarchy. Marie was the older, sensible one. She rallied everyone and made sure we did what was asked of us when Mum needed help. When she was older she would babysit. Jo and Marie argued. They were super-competitive and the arguments would sometimes escalate to major rows. Paul and I would often stir them up, sometimes we'd laugh at them, sometimes we'd know to keep well out of the way. We found it hard to believe at times that two girls could become so animated over things we weren't bothered about, such as hairbrushes and shampoo.

Paul and I fought too. There was also a healthy competitiveness between us. We would strive to outdo each other. If I managed forty keepie-uppies with a football, Paul would spend hours trying to beat the record and if he managed to drive an apple from the tree in the garden over next door's roof with a golf club, I'd practise until I could get it further. Many evenings we'd be called in for dinner and one or other of us would remain outside in the dusk practising repeatedly until we'd broken whatever record it was that had been set that day.

My tussles with Paul were, however, nothing compared with the fights he had with Mattie. He would wind up our younger brother. In return, Mattie would stitch up Paul. If Paul gave Mattie a gentle dig, Mattie would fall over crying in front of our parents like an overly dramatic Italian football player, screaming in mock agony. He was famous for it, but it was fair enough since he was the youngest boy. Mattie would annoy Paul and Rosie would boss Mattie around, despite the fact she was the youngest. Mattie had very bad asthma and Rosie would mother him. They were like an old married couple. It was hilarious to watch, but must have annoyed Mattie no end.

'Mattie, get your jumper!'

'Mattie, have you got your inhaler?'

'Mattie, where are your glasses?'

Poor Mattie couldn't escape. He was surrounded.

If you asked my siblings what they thought of me, they would probably say I was the dull, sensible one. I tried to keep out of the arguments and I tried to remain diplomatic. There was always so much going on and different allegiances being forged and broken that I often found it was best to stay out of it altogether. I'd wander off and read a book or do some colouring. But I wouldn't have changed it for the world. A big family undoubtedly throws up challenges, but we all knew that whenever the chips were down everyone would close ranks and stick together.

Mum and Dad managed to give everyone equal love and attention although Mattie was possibly more spoilt than the rest of us. He was the pet. And because he was ill with asthma a lot, he tended to play on his frailties.

It was easy to be mischievous in such a large household because there was always someone else to blame. At Christmas the annual Advent calendar raid became a Forkan family tradition. Each of us would secretly raid someone else's calendar, open the doors of it and eat all the chocolate. It didn't matter whose. Then, when the crime was uncovered, the guilty party would blame someone else. No one really knew who the culprit was and, over the years, the calendars became a free-for-all.

Collectively as brothers we would terrorize our older sister's boyfriends, making sure we'd play the part of annoying younger siblings in stereotypical detail. We'd intrude on their privacy, snigger if they held hands and generally make nuisances of ourselves.

We'd play practical jokes on each other and, unfortunately, Mattie was often the butt of the pranks. Once, Paul and I tied him to a tree in the back garden. It wasn't too long before Mum noticed he was missing, and rescued him from our idiocy. On another occasion Paul and I decided to convert the garden shed into a Wendy house and rounded up as many tins of paint as we could find. We spent hours inside and locked Mattie in with us as we painted. It was really thoughtless of us, as we enjoyed painting while Mattie sat on the floor breathing the hazardous fumes into his fragile lungs, wheezing and wondering why he wasn't being allowed out. When Mum realized we'd risked causing him to have an asthma attack, she hit the roof. We would have water fights all the time. We would take turns ganging up on each other. Looking back, I know it could all get a bit silly, but really we were just kids having fun.

We weren't allowed a cat or dog because of his condition, so we got the safest things we could: goldfish. We had two of them, named Sharky and George after the TV cartoon. Mattie loved those fish and when they died we told him they had gone on holiday to a fish farm.

'They are in a fish spa and having a really good time,' we lied after they had been flushed down the toilet.

Mattie believed the story wholeheartedly and we perpetuated it for years, keeping him hanging on to the hope that, one day, Sharky and George would return from their holidays. When the penny dropped and he finally realized they weren't coming back, he was really upset.

Although we were looked after and there were house rules governing behaviour, we were also left to make our own entertainment. Mum and Dad both worked and didn't have the time to constantly pamper us with attention. One summer, after Dad had completed some DIY, there was a pile of roofing felt left in the garden so my cousin and I collected it all up and decided to make a bonfire with it. The blaze turned into an inferno within minutes and the flames singed a couple of trees. Future bonfires at the Forkan household were carefully controlled by an adult.

Mattie shared Mum's passion for arts and crafts and had a keen imagination. He watched the movie *Space Jam* one day and got so engrossed in the storyline that he believed, like one of the characters and as the theme tune suggested, he could fly. Paul and I did nothing to discourage his belief, we may even have encouraged it; I've conveniently forgotten! Anyhow, we were in the lounge downstairs when we heard Mattie singing 'I Believe I Can Fly' on the upstairs hall landing in his angelic young voice. There was a short pause followed by a thud at the bottom of the staircase as Mattie painfully discovered that he couldn't.

There was always something going on in the house or, more often, in the garden. From a very young age we were expected to be outside. If it wasn't raining and we weren't at school, we were told to go out and play. We had a television but it was rarely watched and wouldn't get turned on until the evening.

'Why are you sitting in here, go outside and play,' was Dad's mantra if he caught any of us loafing around indoors.

The garden became our playground and we utilized whatever we could find in it – such as roofing felt. We were always encouraged to play sport and were a sporty family so there was always equipment lying around, be it cricket bats and stumps or tennis racquets. We played golf in the garden with apples or pinged them with tennis racquets.

Our back garden gate and back door were always open. The house was rarely locked. If we went away for a few days, our parents would make a big deal about locking the doors. It was like a ceremony.

'We're locking the doors now, kids,' they would announce. 'Last chance to get anything you need or go to the toilet.'

While we were encouraged to be active, we weren't enrolled in countless clubs. Paul and I played cricket for a local side and I was in the Cub Scouts, which I enjoyed, but that was it.

Dad took an active role in the Scouts too. One night we turned up to discover that our Scout leader had quit. After the session, parents were called in and asked if anyone would be willing to volunteer to take his place and lead the troop. I waited outside in the car. When the meeting was over, Dad strolled towards me with a smile on his face.

'Guess who your new leader is, Rob?' he asked.

I went through a few names.

'James's dad? John's dad?'

Dad shook his head.

'No, it's me,' he laughed.

It wasn't something he had professed an interest in and I thought it was hilarious.

'How did you get them to back you?' I asked.

'Well, they asked me what skills I had that I could teach you lads,' he explained. 'And I told them I am going to teach you all how to sit on the toilet and read a paper.'

From then on Dad became the Scout leader and would guide

the pack each week. I couldn't help but laugh when I saw him in his uniform for the first time. He wore a Scout scarf and woggle and a green shirt, the whole get-up. Despite his vow to teach us the art of lazing on the toilet, he took his duties seriously and made a good leader.

Mum was equally as involved in the wider community as Dad. She would regularly help with school events and helped organize a big street party for the anniversary of VE Day. She hosted the fancy-dress contest at the party and made us all costumes. We won. I went as a pinball wizard and my costume was a masterpiece. It was a wizard's outfit with a functioning pinball machine sewn into the front of it which Mum crafted from two wooden vegetable boxes. She loved doing it and her attention to detail and love of design rubbed off on us in later life.

Dad taught us the rules of all the sports he was interested in and played, from football to tennis and golf. We had a pitching wedge at home and Paul and I would use the house opposite for target practice. It must have been one hundred feet away and every so often one of us would hit a practice ball perfectly. As it came down, it would strike one of the windows. They never smashed, we used light balls, but the guy who lived in the house would go mad and come round to complain to Dad who would never believe him.

'They've been at it again, Kevin!' he would rant.

'How could two little boys hit a ball all the way from over here?' Dad would reply. We'd hide upstairs, laughing.

Our lack of formal training in most of the sports we enjoyed meant that when it came to football and tennis we were not the most technically gifted players. We still managed to beat people who were coached, however, because we had very good coordination and were very competitive.

Our lives revolved around being physically active. We didn't have computers or games consoles. We had sports equipment. We made whatever we had last. We had a set of spring-loaded cricket stumps that lasted for about five years and when things broke or we outgrew them, we used them for something else. When we outgrew the swing we broke the seat off it and turned it into a goal.

We learned to improvise. One summer we got a heavy garden roller from somewhere and rolled a patch of the garden as flat as we could. We mowed the lawn short and painted a tennis court on it with white emulsion, using a yard stick to measure it out. We put up a couple of posts from B & Q on either side of the court and Mum made a net to string between them. Subsequently we had our own tennis court.

Our parents believed wholeheartedly that things had to be earned. We were never given money without doing something in exchange for it. If we wanted something, we had to do chores or find ways to earn money to pay for it. Mum and Dad worked hard for what we had and we appreciated what we were given. Although we did not go without, we were never spoilt and often, when times were not so profitable, we were expected to make do with what we had.

One year we got a tree house because our parents couldn't afford to take us on holiday. Dad was rubbish at DIY and couldn't build one from scratch, so he bought one from a garden centre. It was six-foot high and on stilts; a proper cabin, the wood on the outside still had bark on it. There was a veranda around it.

'We're not going away this year,' Mum and Dad announced when they unveiled it, 'so you can have this instead and enjoy it all summer.'

The house became a social hub for other kids in the area because the garden was so well equipped and the back gate was always open. Everyone was welcome, our parents didn't mind.

While our neighbours had lawns as pristine as the turf at Old Trafford, with beautiful borders stocked with flowers and fish ponds with Koi carp in them, in comparison, after years of battering by six children, our garden looked ramshackle; but that just added to the charm.

Having such a large family did present challenges to our parents, although they never complained. When Mum first settled into motherhood, she enjoyed cooking but by the time the sixth child had come along and we had grown up, the enjoyment of preparing so much food started to wear thin. Dad helped, he enjoyed cooking too, but eventually the process of feeding so many children became an almost industrial process.

Mum was also very artistic and good at DIY. She was carefree and a free spirit. She would spend hours with us making dough sculptures, and one year she made Rosie a doll's house complete with furniture, all from craft materials. She could make anything. She tried her best to make the house look pretty and was very good at creating things, but it ended up being quite functional instead. After a few years of us traipsing in and out from the garden, the carpet was replaced with laminate flooring, which was easier to clean, and the walls were splashed with plain emulsion to cover the scuff marks and the occasional crayon scrawl.

There was also the issue of transporting so many children. It was a struggle to get us all together in a single vehicle until Dad had a stroke of luck. Although he wasn't a gambling man, each year he would allow himself a flutter on the Grand National. He knew very little about horses, just the basics – that they had four legs and they ran fast – but one year he decided that he'd try his hand at an accumulator. Amazingly, his selection came in thanks to the winning horse, Papillon. Dad won a tidy sum. He was over the moon. With the money he bought a second-hand Mercedes minibus. It was a good runner, if a little run-down, and Mum decorated it by putting on her own butterfly design transfers. The vehicle was christened Papillon and became the family run-around.

Although the showroom did well for many years, the car trade suffered badly in the recession in the early nineties and Dad's business sadly folded. Mum and Dad were optimistic throughout, however. They were great believers that you make your own luck in life. They were very positive people and Dad saw the closure of one chapter of his life as an opportunity to open another. In business terms he was a visionary. He was always coming up with new ideas and he set about building a new company: Rose Fashions. The idea was ahead of its time and it was a proper family affair that would influence Paul and me many years later.

Rose Fashions was a social enterprise at a time when no one really knew what a social enterprise was. It worked well in the austere climate of the time when, for many people, money for luxuries was tight. The concept was simple. Mum and Dad made contacts with high-street clothes retailers and bought seconds, over-ordered stock and ends of lines from them at a big discount.

They would then contact schools, hospitals, charities and other community organizations and offer to host fashion shows for them at which ticket holders would be able to buy the clothes being displayed by the models.

The events were social occasions. The organizations backing them were able to set up bars and sell food and drink in the venues they provided, so they made money from ticket sales and refreshments while my parents made money from the sale of their stock. Everyone was happy.

They worked incredibly hard booking shows in and around the Home Counties, organizing models and sourcing stock. They did mail shots and telephone canvassing. The shows took place in school halls, university buildings, leisure centres and community centres. The organizations loved them because they provided good fundraising opportunities. The clothes on sale were from well-known high street retailers and were sold at a fraction of the high-street price and so ticket holders benefited too. Some nights there would be up to 1,000 people at the shows.

Although the business started small, it soon grew. Our parents approached it with the same enthusiasm they afforded most opportunities in life. They immersed themselves in it and as a family we all got involved, helping size stock and stuff envelopes with promotional material.

Each night there would be three or four shows going on in and around the area we lived in. Initially the business started in the house but, as it grew, Dad bought a new office: a Portakabin school classroom that one of the schools nearby no longer needed. Dad had the building dismantled and erected in the back garden. When the business outgrew its Portakabin HQ and moved to a warehouse in the nearby town of Coulsdon, we were allowed to use the hut as a den, which was paradise.

The challenges of having so many children never seemed to weigh down on our parents. Childhood was as close to idyllic as it could have been. We had ups and downs like everyone, but we were furnished with the right attitude to weather the challenges and we valued our freedoms and the opportunities we were given. We were decent, sociable kids. Kevin and Sandra had done well.

CHAPTER 2

Our Journey Begins

OF COURSE, WHILE life afforded us a lot of fun, there was also school to attend, which I didn't mind. I went to Woodcote Primary School in nearby Coulsdon and then, at eleven, I went to Woodcote High School: the local comprehensive. Dad's stories about his travels must have rubbed off on me as I enjoyed learning about the world. I was naturally inquisitive and particularly enjoyed finding out about other countries and cultures. I wasn't great at maths and English but I liked history, geography and religious education. Like Mum, I also enjoyed art; all of us did.

Mum and Dad encouraged us to learn, but not solely for academic achievement. We knew from early on that work was important and that in life, if you wanted to get by, you had to rely just as much on your wits and drive as you did on your ability to read, write and do sums. We all realized on some subconscious level that in life you get a long way on determination and guile. We saw it every day in the way Mum and Dad devoted themselves to their business. They were hard workers and as Rose Fashions grew, it became the focus of their lives. They organized the shows from our house and most nights of the week people would come and go, collecting stock and materials. The models who wore the clothes also set off from the house so several nights a week groups of attractive girls and ladies would arrive.

When she was older, Marie got some of her friends involved and some of the yummy mummies from our school also signed up to earn a bit of extra money. Paul and I were too young to appreciate this at first, but as we grew older we increasingly found excuses to help out. Our envious friends were always quick to remind us how lucky we were having a procession of hot girls coming in and out of the house.

I didn't know what the term entrepreneurial spirit meant when I was ten, but I understood that Dad had ideas and that he made them work. Rose Fashions started from nothing and grew into a very profitable business. The house was a buzzing hub of enterprise and I watched and learned, absorbing some of that entrepreneurial spirit by osmosis. One of the tasks I enjoyed most during my time at school was a project in which pupils were required to design, make and market their own brands. I loved the chance to take a concept and create something tangible from an idea. I made sweets. They were truffles. I designed and made packaging and developed a sales strategy. Apart from reading, writing and learning to count, it was probably the most valuable thing I ever did at school. I've not used algebra to this day and sometimes I wondered what the point was in what we were learning. The lessons and life skills Mum and Dad were teaching us – common sense, independence, resilience – seemed much more relevant.

Outside school, Paul and I were always on the lookout for ways to earn money. We didn't expect it to be handed to us. We knocked on doors and washed cars in the neighbourhood. During one summer holiday, along with a friend, I made a decent amount of money. I had it stuffed in a box under my bed. We targeted the roads with the big houses. I was twelve and, looking back, I'm sure Dad must have been suspicious of the origins of such a large haul of cash.

Mum and Dad encouraged us to think for ourselves and, even though they were always busy, they still found time to help and support us with advice. They were not absent parents. They'd take us to cricket, they'd take us out and they stretched themselves and eked out as much time as they could to make sure they were a constant presence in our lives. They would work in the evenings and be around in the days. They worked round the clock at weekends and juggled their hours so one of them was always on hand should we need to go somewhere. And they allowed us to have our friends round as much as we wanted. It wasn't like a normal home. There was always something going on and, to this day, my mates from childhood tell me what a fun place our house was.

Random stuff happened there, usually as a result of a parental whim. For example, one afternoon Dad arrived home with a bouncy castle in the back of the car. A local leisure centre had shut down and was throwing it out so Dad offered to take it off their hands. He dumped it in the back garden and said, 'There you go, kids.' We inflated it with the blower that came with it. It was huge and had a big inflatable clown's head at the front. You could see it from several gardens away when it was fully inflated so when the clown's head rose over Purley, all the local kids knew it was bouncy castle time at the Forkans'. It was like Disneyland, but in Croydon!

That bouncy castle got a lot of use. We put it under the second-floor windows and jumped out onto it. We got hosepipes and Fairy Liquid and had foam parties. Between us we had a lot of friends and the garden would end up crowded with loads of teenage girls and a load of young lads having apple fights, jumping on the bouncy castle and climbing trees.

When we were given the Portakabin, it became akin to a local youth club for us and our friends. We decorated it and found furniture for it. It was fully weatherproofed, insulated and heated and had lights and power. When she got older, Marie moved into it and made it her bedroom.

There was always a lot of fun and laughter in the house. Mum was a practical joker and was always playing pranks on us and Dad. We were also taught to be creative. Mum would spend hours drawing with us and teaching us how to make things and be creative ourselves.

She was also very musical, a trait that Rosie picked up. Mum loved karaoke. She loved a bit of Celine Dion and *Grease*. During staff nights out, she was always the first on the mic and the last off.

While I didn't mind school, it was a different story for Paul. He struggled. He had trouble reading and lagged behind the other children. He became frustrated and his behaviour suffered.

He was not academic and just couldn't get on with the learning by rote system used in schools. There was some form of mental block there that he just couldn't seem to overcome. To their credit, Mum and Dad did not pressure him. There was obviously an issue which needed to be addressed because Paul was a bright kid. He picked things up and understood things, but when it came to reading and writing, something just would not click.

Eventually he was diagnosed with dyslexia. Once we knew, it was obvious. Paul's brain had trouble processing words, letters and symbols. He would see and write letters and numbers back to front. The condition didn't affect his general intelligence and that was what frustrated him. He wanted to learn, but the way he was taught made it hard for him and that in turn aggravated him. In primary school he was assigned a teaching assistant who would sit with him in class and work with him. At one stage he was given a pair of special glasses to wear with coloured lenses as a certain type of dyslexia can be exacerbated by a white background.

As he got older, he became rebellious. He did things such as set off fire alarms in school and was the joker in the class. On one occasion he dyed his hair blue and white, the colours of the team we all supported: QPR. He sometimes got sent home from school for bad behaviour. But underneath it all he was a good kid and felt misunderstood. Mum and Dad were patient; they realized how tough school life was for him.

Dad tried different things to help. He read up on the condition to find out what solutions there were. He once read in a paper that travel sickness pills could help and got Paul to take them. The theory behind the treatment was that dyslexia affects the parts of the brain involved in movement or balance rather than those controlling thought and language. According to the report there was some scientific evidence to support the idea that travel sickness pills could help, although it didn't seem to help Paul.

Mum and Dad coped well with Paul's situation and understood the underlying issues. They'd been through the mill with Mattie and his asthma so were unperturbed by Paul and his behavioural and learning issues. In life, Mum and Dad always approached problems positively, pragmatically and stoically.

Mattie's asthma did not improve as he got older. It seemed to get worse. He was in and out of hospital. He was not as energetic and sporty as Paul and me because he couldn't be. His asthma attacks were sparked by many triggers. Cold weather, changes in temperature, pollen, dust, animals; they were all potentially dangerous for him. The condition was chronic and Mattie was on a range of medication to try and control it. He had several different types of inhaler and was hooked up to a nebulizer most nights. We had oxygen tanks in the house for him. The medication meant he grew slowly. Despite the age gap between him and Rosie, by the time he was in primary school he was not much taller than his younger sister.

When he had an attack it was terrifying. He would turn pale, his lips would go blue and he struggled for breath as his lungs closed up. Mum and Dad were well aware of the signs and triggers and kept a close eye on him.

Mattie's condition had one advantage for us all though. He was particularly prone to severe attacks in cold conditions and so, when our parents could afford it, we would go on holiday in the winter time. We did normal package tours to places such as Tenerife and Majorca and our parents saved hard. We were a family of eight so holidays were expensive. In the years when we couldn't afford a foreign holiday, we went to places such as the Isle of Wight and stayed in holiday parks.

One year, when the business was doing particularly well, our parents decided to go further afield and booked our first long-haul holiday. They chose the island of St Kitts in the Caribbean. We couldn't afford to stay in five-star luxury and that suited everyone. Mum and Dad were not the sort of couple who needed to be surrounded by creature comforts. We stayed in a lower-budget hotel that was clean and friendly.

It was the first time I had ever been anywhere exotic and we were all spellbound by the white sand and crystal-clear blue sea, fringed by lush forest. It was as close to paradise as I'd ever seen and I spent most days snorkelling, wide-eyed, staring at the colourful fish beneath the waves.

Mum and Dad liked to swim too, but more than that they enjoyed sunbathing. They worked hard so they made the most of the opportunity to relax. Dad, however, relaxed a little too much and burned himself in the intense tropical sun. He turned as red as a lobster and looked like a typical Brit abroad.

One of the coconut sellers on the beach noticed his glowing complexion and discomfort one day and approached him as he sat under a sunshade.

'That looks very painful, sir,' he commented. 'Try applying some of this.'

He handed Dad a large, thick slab of plantlife. A jelly-like ooze was bulging from the open end where the chunk had been cut from the plant.

'Rub that on your skin,' the man advised.

Dad did and was amazed at how his scorched skin felt immediately cooler.

'It's called Aloe Vera,' the man explained.

We all had a go and the man was right. It was like air con for the skin. It was amazing.

It was the mid-nineties and none of us had heard of this miraculous Aloe Vera plant. Ever the entrepreneur, in his sunburned agony Dad spotted a business opportunity.

For the rest of the day he discussed it with Mum and they formulated a plan. While we were still on holiday, they found a supplier who manufactured Aloe Vera toiletries and they commissioned the company to manufacture a batch of aftersun lotion for them. They decided to create their own brand and ship the lotion to the UK where it could be sold at the fashion shows in the summer. They even got the lotion tested at a lab in St Kitts and in the UK to make sure it was clinically safe to use. In the space of a two-week holiday they diversified from fashion into the beauty business.

Soon after we arrived back home from the holiday, the first batch of Forkan Aloe Vera Aftersun arrived at the house from the Caribbean. Mum designed a logo for it using Microsoft Clipart; she chose a sun, but turned it green to signify the Aloe Vera plant; it was pretty basic stuff, branding by numbers. She printed out hundreds of labels and we were put to work sticking them on the clear plastic bottles that the product was shipped in. Quality control was not as stringent in those first shipments as it possibly could have been and some of the labels went on smeared and wonky.

It was a good idea but, in all honesty, it looked rubbish, like something I might have created in my school project. Still, our parents persevered and the following summer Mum went to Ibiza with some of the models who worked on the fashion shows and took a suitcase full of the lotion with her. The group spent a week pounding the beaches selling and promoting the brand. Despite their efforts it never really took off.

As well as providing a business opportunity, that long-haul trip to the West Indies reawakened my father's interest in travel. The following Christmas we went to Gran Canaria, but Dad couldn't shake the feeling that he wanted to go further afield. Perhaps he realized that it wasn't such a chore travelling distances with a young family. We'd all coped with the flight and jet lag fine and took the change in climate and culture in our stride. Mum also harboured an ambition to go further afield. She had never travelled and was open to new experiences.

To this day, I'm not sure what their motivations really were, but the year after we went to Gran Canaria, when I was thirteen, they put the house on the market. They didn't seem to be in a hurry to find somewhere else to move to either. I think the plan was to reassess their lives and to see what options were open to them and, if need be, to rent somewhere while they made up their minds. We didn't question it; after all, we were just children.

While the sale of the house was going through, they booked our next winter break: to India. I was more excited about the holiday than the move. I knew very little about India and when I told my mates at school, who spent their holidays in Disneyland or the Med, they laughed.

'What are you going there for? There's nothing to do and everyone lives in mud huts.'

In his travels Dad hadn't been to Asia and fancied seeing it, so our parents got a cheap last-minute deal from Teletext to the beach resort of Goa.

We quickly had our typhoid jabs, Dad bought a copy of the Lonely Planet travel guide and, after breaking up from school, the eight of us jetted off to the other side of the world to experience the Indian subcontinent.

It is fair to say that, when we landed, our lives took a turn in a new direction. None of us had ever experienced anything like it. From the moment we walked out of the airport, India was in our faces: loud, colourful, chaotic, hot and wondrous. It was amazing. It smelled like no other place. The people were both friendly and crazy. There were a billion people all trying to live in a place the size of Europe; it was in parts crammed and in other parts an open wilderness. It was an extraordinary melting pot where different religions, cultures and castes – Hindus, Christians, Muslims and Buddhists – all managed to exist together in a humidity that hung round you like a wet towel that assaulted the senses.

Out of the airport terminal, the first thing we noticed were the beggars and the hawkers. Everyone crowded round us, kids and adults. They were like vultures. They tried to grab our bags in order to carry them for us, in exchange for money, but we didn't know who to trust. Our parents tried to watch all six of us while keeping an eye on the mob who were surrounding us and the hands that were trying to grasp our suitcases. Taxi drivers tried ushering us into their vehicles. It was a relief when we spotted the transfer bus that was taking us to the accommodation we'd booked.

The relief did not last for long. The ride to the hotel was insane. When the bus pulled out of the car park into the road system, Paul and I sat with jaws agape staring at the madness that engulfed us. There were people everywhere and most of them seemed to have a death wish. People on bicycles played chicken with lorries, children wandered into the paths of cars, and hundreds of mopeds zipped through tiny gaps in the traffic, buzzing like angry wasps. And randomly, every few hundred yards, a donkey, horse or cow would amble into the melee.

'What the hell is going on here?' I thought to myself. The chaos was unsettling. I was nervous and excited at the same time. Cars would come at the coach head-on and then tuck into a tiny gap in the traffic at the last second. Horns blared. People shouted. There was no order. It was manic.

When we left the centre of town, the journey took us through parts of forests where the road was just a dusty track. Every few yards the bus lurched to the left or right as the driver swerved to avoid huge potholes. People sat precariously by the side of the road selling fruit or other goods. It was like we'd gone back a hundred years. It was my first taste of the developing world and I did not know whether to laugh or cry. Where had our parents taken us?

Our destination, Goa, was in the west of the country. Back then it was still underdeveloped in terms of tourist amenities. It was predominantly a hippy resort. It was known among travellers for its beaches and historic sites. It was also very cheap. You could eat out for less than a pound and basic accommodation was just a few pounds per night.

Goa had been colonized by the Portuguese after traders landed there in the sixteenth century and a lot of Portuguese influences could still be seen in its architecture. We stayed near the beach in a place called Beira Mar, which was a small hotel complex with a pool and restaurant and looked like something you'd find at the lower end of the accommodation spectrum in the Algarve. I shared a room with Paul. In it there were two beds, a fan and a toilet. It was basic, with no frills, but that was all we needed because we were out most of the time anyway.

We were there for two weeks and every day was filled with new experiences and activities. We went to a zoo and saw animals we'd never seen before. It was quite an experience as when the animals were fed, they were fed live food. The big cats were fed live chickens and the reptiles were fed live rats. I remember seeing a terrified, sweating rat cowering in the corner of a glass tank because it knew it was going to get eaten by the snake coiled patiently in the corner, waiting to strike. There was an elephant chained to a tree which looked distressed. It was huge and could easily have pulled the tree out of the ground. Like a lot of things in India, cruelty and wonder were two sides of the same coin. It was that clash of beauty and horror that made the place so intoxicating. Many of the beggars we saw were disabled. Some had missing limbs, others were disfigured or suffering from disease. It was shocking. We saw children working by the side of the road selling fruit and others begging on the beaches.

But beneath the surface, as we got used to the alien sights and sounds, there was a friendly feel to the place. The people were warm and accommodating.

Health and safety rules were not as stringent as they were back home. On one trip we visited spectacular waterfalls and swam in the freshwater pools below them. A railway ran around the top of the huge falls, precariously balanced on the cliffs. Locals told us that the line had the dubious honour of being christened the most dangerous stretch of railway in the world. The twists and turns were so sharp in places that each year a train full of passengers would inevitably take a turn too fast, tip over and plunge down the ravine. We had a tour guide for the trip and he encouraged us to drink the water from the pools that people were swimming in.

'Very clean, good for you,' he explained. We declined and stuck to our bottled water.

At night we ate either in the hotel or at local restaurants on the beach. Mum and Dad never did fully inclusive; they believed if you went somewhere, you explored and ate where the locals ate. Delhi Belly was simply part of the experience, although we all managed to dodge that particular bullet. There were a few pizza joints dotted around the town and an Italian restaurant staffed entirely by Indians who used local ingredients and a fair degree of culinary ingenuity to create 'authentic' Italian dishes, but we ate mainly Indian or Nepalese food, which was delicious.

We visited stunning temples. Mum and Dad were not religious but they were interested in spirituality and culture. We looked at some of the wildlife. We chilled out on the beach and by the pool. We swam in the warm, clear blue sea and bought a cricket set to play with on the beach. India is a cricket-mad nation and, as soon as we set up, some of the local kids came to watch. We played matches with the beach kids who worked in the shacks selling snacks and fruit juice.

One day Mum and Dad decided to take us to a local children's home. Mum, especially, had never tried to shy away from the poverty in the country. She had a keen sense of social justice and frequently reminded us how lucky we were. There was a charity operating in and around Goa that looked after orphaned children and our parents had been speaking to one of its volunteers. The volunteer invited them along and they decided that it would be beneficial for us to see how less fortunate people lived. Mum and Dad were very thoughtful and philanthropic and they believed it would help us in life to realize how lucky we were. They wanted to show us the other side of the world, even on holiday. So we went along to the home and met some of the children there. It was just a brief visit but we did leave with a different perspective. We all thought about those children afterwards. It was hard to comprehend what being orphaned was like for them. It's not a situation any child should be in but, tragically, it happens. Perhaps that short visit made us appreciate our own parents even more.

The day before we left to return home, we said goodbye to the beach kids we'd met and gave them our football shirts and cricket set. We said goodbye to India but carried a little bit of it back with us. Many people who travel there say that although it can be a cruel and shocking country, it also gets under your skin and while it can be a frustrating place, it also enchants you. Our parents were enchanted by it. They had fallen in love with the place and the people. And when we got back, they started making plans.

CHAPTER 3

Expanding Horizons

MUM AND DAD seized opportunities. They did not let life pass them by. In business Dad would turn his hand to anything he thought might work, like the Aloe Vera lotion. He followed his instincts, he had a keen sense of right and wrong and he was inquisitive. He had a 'you only live once, make the most of it' attitude. And he did.

India sparked something in him and also in Mum. I think they had an epiphany while they were there and realized it was time for a change. He also wanted to show us the world and to expand our horizons. He wasn't academic, but he knew enough to know that school didn't have the answers to everything. It was his belief that we would become better, more rounded humans if we experienced the world and we were not going to do that sitting in a classroom in Croydon.

We returned from India and Mum and Dad's lives were at a crossroads. They had a buyer for the house and no firm plans for what to do next. They had lived in the same home for twenty years and had raised us there. There was a lot of equity in the property and they did not want to rush to make decisions about where to invest it. Marie and Jo were older, it wouldn't be long before we all started moving out and flying the nest, so they were reticent about buying another large house and settling back down into the same pattern of life. They had ideas. They even toyed with the possibility of moving to the Caribbean and starting a business exporting log cabins. But India kept calling.

Ultimately I believe they were disillusioned with the rat race. Their business had been a big success and had provided them with a comfortable living, but they had paid a price. The hours were long. They had been working flat out for many years, in addition to raising a large family. They would work six or seven days a week because when you work in your own business you never really switch off. They would get home at midnight from a show, have dinner and be up first thing in the morning to start all over again. Even when you love what you do, that cycle can become repetitive. Business had also started to slow. The recession was lifting, people were buying clothes online, there were cheaper outlets. There was now a lot of competition. They yearned for a change of pace and scenery.

The sale of the house and the holiday in India created a perfect storm. For the first time in many years, they felt they had the freedom to do something different and they decided: 'Screw it! Let's broaden our horizons!'

I'm not sure how long they had been thinking about taking the radical path they did. To me it seems like it was a quick decision, but perhaps they had been mulling it over for years and took us all to India on holiday as a test to see how we coped and whether we liked it. In the weeks after we came back, they kept dropping hints.

'So what did you think of it over there?'

'Did you like it?'

'Would you ever like to go back?'

It was January and the start of a new school term when the subject came up again. We were all sitting in the lounge together one night.

'How would you feel if we told you we were thinking of moving to India for a few months to go travelling around?' Mum asked.

We were surprised and excited.

'Really?' I asked.

'It's an idea,' she said.

I asked about school and she explained that we could be home-schooled. She would teach us as we travelled. It seemed like a crazy idea but a good one to me. At that age you don't question your parents and you trust their judgement.

Opinions in the rest of the family were split. Paul, Mattie and Rosie liked the idea. Mattie and Rosie were young and naturally followed our parents' lead anyway. Mattie was a mummy's boy and Rosie loved adventure. She had become a tomboy over the years because she hung around with her three older brothers, rather than her sisters. She couldn't play with the older girls because the age gap was so big so she ended up climbing trees and getting into scrapes with us.

Marie and Jo were less sure. They had enjoyed the holiday but were not so enamoured of the prospect of travelling for several months in a country where amenities could be basic to say the least. Both were older and had boyfriends and jobs which they did not want to leave so the idea of roughing it did not appeal to them.

As the days went on, our parents became increasingly certain and we became increasingly excited. They discussed matters with our older sisters, offered to pay for them to travel independently if they wanted and offered help with accommodation if they chose to stay in the UK. The girls decided they wanted to move in with their boyfriends. Our nan was prepared to help out too. Mum and Dad told Paul and me to go into school and explain to our teachers that we were leaving to go and live in India for a while.

That was one of the best and most bizarre conversations I ever had with my teachers.

'My parents said to tell you I'm leaving school. I'm going to live in India!' I explained.

The teachers didn't believe me, but the reality of the situation was that there was very little the education authorities could do. They couldn't make us stay if we were moving abroad.

Although it seemed like a spur-of-the moment decision, the time was right. I had only been at secondary school for eighteen months, Paul was yet to start and was struggling at school anyway and Mattie and Rosie were young; they would benefit more from travel than they would from being in a classroom.

The wider family were told and thought our parents were crazy. Initially they thought it was a joke. Then, when they realized it wasn't, they were shocked. It seemed so random and quick. We had only been back from holiday for a few weeks and there we were, getting ready to become a family of travellers. Our aunts, uncles and grandparents were dead against it. They questioned why our parents were doing it and maintained that we needed to stay in school and get an education. Perhaps they would have understood if it was France or Spain, but India? It was ludicrous, they said; a pipe dream. But they had already worked out that ours was the eccentric, out-of-the-box family. We had never done anything by the rules and it really didn't matter what they thought. Once Mum and Dad decided to do something, it was hard to talk them out of it. If you told Dad he couldn't do something, he would do it out of stubbornness to prove you wrong. It is a quality we all developed ourselves over the years. We didn't pay much attention to people, especially naysayers.

For my part, I didn't worry one bit. When you are a kid, you don't. I wasn't concerned. I didn't think there would be dangers. I was excited. You assume that if your parents are doing it, then it must be OK. They led the way and they never seemed worried so we followed.

Rose Fashions was wound up, the house sale went through and we had a mass clear-out. It was almost like cleansing our lives of the possessions we had. Most of it was given away to family, friends and charity. We weren't a family that surrounded ourselves with lots of stuff but most of what we had would be useless where we were going and if it didn't work out there and we came back we could always buy new things. It was only stuff, after all.

'You can take one bag each and whatever you want to take, you carry yourself,' explained Dad. We were travelling light. India was so cheap we could replace most things anyhow. My luxury items were a tennis racquet and a cricket bat. Paul took football shirts. The valuables we decided to keep were put in storage for when we eventually decided to come back.

When it was time to leave, I said goodbye to my friends. I had a few groups of close mates; I still see them now. One was a group of lads from high school: Craig, James and Dean. There was a pack of us. We all liked sport. We were also pals with a couple of lads whose gardens backed onto ours: Mark and Dom. They loved football, bike rides and water fights. There was also an Italian family nearby with two kids, Steph and Sandro, who we were friends with. Their uncle set up the Costa Coffee chain. Our parents allowed us to have a final party and sleepover in the Portakabin. Someone managed to get hold of a load of cans of lager and we drank them and stuffed the empties into a bin liner and hid it under the cabin assuming, as we were leaving, our parents wouldn't know and they'd be left for the new owners to find. But Mattie uncovered them and told our parents, who gave us a massive telling-off.

It was emotional when we left the house. There was a lifetime full of memories in it and it must have been even harder for our parents as it was their first and only family home together. They had raised six children in it. But that told me they were one hundred per cent sure of what they were doing. They had the taste for travel and adventure. Mum had never travelled and she wanted to see the world, so we all said goodbye to our suburban life, bid our sisters farewell at the airport and in early 2001 we boarded a plane back to India just a few weeks after we'd returned from our first trip there.

We were going back to Goa to stay in Beira Mar. There was a villa in the grounds with enough space to house a large family, so Mum and Dad had rented that and it was to become our base. We planned to stay there but take long trips to other parts of the country for weeks at a time.

On the flight we had a stopover in Jordan and spent a couple of days there, visiting the ancient site of Petra, which was amazing. From there we flew into Mumbai because it worked out cheaper and, from Mumbai airport, we hired a driver to take us on the eighteen-hour trip to the villa. It was a ride even more nail-biting than our first experience on India's roads, made worse by the fact that the driver decided to do it without stopping. The vehicle was a large people carrier and the route took us through beautiful mountains. We couldn't enjoy the scenery, however, because the driver kept falling asleep. He only stopped to eat or for toilet breaks and at one point went into a chemist and came out with pills he took to keep him awake. Mum stayed awake too, terrified that the man at the wheel would drop off and send us all careering off the road. She couldn't relax and organized us in a rota to keep the driver distracted.

'Keep talking to him,' she whispered. 'Do anything to keep him awake.'

So for the best part of the journey we terrorized the man, flicking his ears, asking him question after question, singing to him, shouting and generally making a noise.

Dad was having a nightmare journey too. Since the crash he had been involved in when he was in Australia, he had developed a phobia of road bridges. He'd get anxious driving over them in the UK and on the journey to Goa, on dangerous roads with a sleepy driver and plunging mountain ravines, that anxiety was amplified. Dad spent half the journey cowering in the seat with a jacket pulled over his head.

Surprisingly we arrived in Goa intact and settled into the villa which was clean and comfortable and had four bedrooms. Mum and Dad had one, Mattie and Rosie had their own rooms and Paul and I shared. At night, the sound of the waves lulled us to sleep.

The house was set back 200 metres from the beach. It had a small garden but we rarely used it. There was a TV in the lounge and we watched football now and then when it was on. Dad watched the BBC news channel to keep up to date with events back home but most of the time we were outside swimming and playing on the beach. There was a bathroom with a shower and a 'proper' toilet, which was a relief. We'd discovered on our first trip that restroom facilities in the country could vary wildly depending on where you were. Sometimes they were just wooden stalls with a hole in the floor. The first time I used one we were eating in a dodgy restaurant. I walked in and thought, 'What the hell . . . ?'

There was also a kitchen with an oven but it was rarely used. We mainly went out to eat. It was so cheap there was little point cooking. It could also be a hassle to prepare food. If you wanted a chicken you'd have to butcher it yourself. You would have to gut it, pluck it and cut its head off, then carve it up. It wasn't worth it and it was always nice to go out, sit together and have a meal as at home we would only go out once in a while because Mum and Dad worked so much.

We were encouraged to explore just as we had been in the UK. There were no excuses for sitting indoors. We had the beach and the weather. We would be out all day playing.

We spent the first week chilling out, acclimatizing and planning. There was a lot to see and we had a wish list of places we wanted to visit. We spoke to travellers staying at the hotel and found out about some of the amazing locations we could go to.

Certain attractions were off limits, however, because of Mattie's asthma. The Taj Mahal was one such place. Pollution levels in Agra, where the palace is located, were dangerously high and it was too risky to take our youngest brother there in case the conditions caused an attack.

I felt at home there straight away. India hooked me in. Most people who go there say it is the best place they've ever been. Until you've been there it is hard to understand because at first it isn't an easy place to experience. It's like you've travelled back in time in certain parts, not just because of the lack of infrastructure and amenities; there are also ancient rules and traditions that still impact on life there. Certain sections of the community are treated badly because of their background, or caste. There is also much poverty, which can be very difficult to witness. The whole culture is completely different. At first you are shocked, but when that passes you are able to see underneath the surface and realize how special it is. Near where we stayed there were treehouses that travellers could rent. They were plain inside with just a light, a fan and a bed. The bed linen was old sheets and guests had to share their accommodation with cockroaches and other undesirable and uninvited wildlife. For some, a night in there would be like a prison sentence. The huts were remote. But at night the stars were so bright they reflected off the sea. The trick to India was often seeing past what was in your face. Once you got past the dodgy sheets and the cockroaches you realized you were actually in paradise on a stunning tropical beach with the freedom to do whatever you wanted.

When we arrived in India, the plan was always to stay for four months and then go back to the UK. The plan soon changed.

We went back to the UK periodically to visit family and friends, but stayed mainly in India for almost four years. Mum and Dad toyed with the idea of travelling further afield. They thought about Australia and New Zealand but, ultimately, India kept calling them back.

CHAPTER 4

Life on the Road

WE GRADUALLY SETTLED into a routine of sorts a few weeks after our arrival. True to her word, Mum attempted to home-school us. Our first lesson took place on the beach by the villa. We sat in the warm sand under an umbrella made of palm fronds. Mum bought some books and we had exercise pads to write in. The sea lapped invitingly at the shoreline a few feet in front of us. It was hard to concentrate. The lessons didn't last long and as we were all at different stages it was hard to keep tabs on who was doing what. Paul lost interest very quickly. I'd often do art and sketch the landscape.

Mum and Dad increasingly immersed themselves in the lifestyle. India is very spiritual and some of the places we visited oozed an almost supernatural atmosphere. We visited amazing temples and holy sites and, even though we were young, we appreciated the sacred wonder of them. We visited Shri Mangeshi Temple, a holy site dedicated to the Hindu deity Lord Shiva. With its colourful and intricate features, the vast site sat in a clearing in the middle of lush forest and was one of the largest temples in Goa. We investigated the buildings: the domed hall, the seven-storey octagonal lamp tower, and felt like explorers in a Hollywood movie.

One day, Dad announced a new addition to our daily routine.

'I'm getting you kids a yoga teacher,' he told us.

'A what?' we sniggered.

'Yoga. It'll help you concentrate and keep you fit,' he promised.

Yoga was big in India. Everyone did it and Dad had been getting increasingly interested in it too; he was a bit of a hippy at heart. The Hindu spiritual discipline had fallen out of favour in the UK after being big in the seventies but for many Indians it was a way of life. For them it was a religious and meditative practice, not just a fitness fad.

A few days after Dad's announcement, a strange-looking man arrived at the villa carrying a rolled-up mat. He was tall and bald with a goatee beard. He wore loose baggy harem pants and a vest. He was wiry and thin and spoke slowly and hypnotically. He was our yoga teacher; half hippy, half guru.

We all lined up in the garden and put beach mats down.

'Raise your arms on the in-breath . . . hold . . . exhale the out-breath,' the man began. His face was a picture of serene contemplation as he contorted himself into an unnatural-looking position.

'Focus on the breath.'

I looked at Paul. He glanced back. Paul started sniggering.

The man switched posture.

'. . . and into Warrior pose,' he instructed dramatically, jutting his chin to the sky.

I started giggling too. Mattie and Rosie cracked and the more we tried not to laugh, the more we did. I tried not to look at Paul, but each time our eyes met we started cracking up.

The serene expression on the man's face broke into a frown.

'Yogic practice needs concentration,' he said.

He persevered through the sniggers and for several weeks he would turn up at the villa and we'd spend the hour laughing at him and taking the mickey while he tried to teach us the art of yoga. We were fresh from Croydon in south London and wore sports kit and football shirts. He was a mystic from the East and wore beads. The culture clash couldn't have been more jarring.

Soon after we first arrived, possibly when it became apparent the home-schooling wouldn't work, we were enrolled in an Indian school. However, because we knew no Hindi and didn't know about the culture and history of the country, we were behind the school syllabus for our year and put down to younger age groups. Paul was around twelve and he was put in a class with eight-year-olds. The school was in an old Victorian colonial building. It was austere and strict. There were no male teachers and the women had to be addressed as 'ma'am'. It was all very old-fashioned and a world away from the Croydon comprehensive I was used to. The head teacher walked around threateningly with a stick and in the morning we did marching drill. It was like going back to Dickensian times. In the playground eighteen-year-olds would be doing hopscotch and skipping. That wouldn't happen in Croydon: they would have grown out of that by year seven and by eighteen some of the girls would have been on their second child!

Uniform was strictly enforced. We wore blue tailored shorts with white shirts. On the two days a week we did PE, we wore the same shorts with a white polo shirt. We had to wear smart polished leather shoes and knee-high socks. I found it funny; it felt like fancy dress at first.

It was a private school and the fees were three pounds a term, way more than average native families could afford. It was top of the range and there were a lot of Western kids there, but not many Brits. Most of them came from eccentric families where the parents had set off on the hippy trail and got lost. One kid in my class had driven with his parents halfway across the globe from the UK in a military vehicle that had been used in the Gulf War. I can only imagine how that might have played out when they crossed the Middle East. They were hard-core travellers. Some of the kids had dreadlocks. I felt sorry for some. One girl was only young and was pregnant by one of the locals. A lot of the kids had assimilated into Indian culture so well they wore Indian jewellery and dressed like locals outside school. Me and Paul always looked Western, however, and dressed in sports casual.

We made friends easily at school. There were pupils from all over Europe, but mostly from Germany and Holland. Many had parents who were working in Goa. We also made friends with some of the kids who worked in the beach shacks and found a local kick-about football team that we played with. At one point an English family with kids moved into the villa next door. Like us they used it as a base and then went travelling around. There were also a few older British couples who had been to Goa on holiday and went back to live there when they retired. A British pension went a long way if you were adventurous enough. Ultimately, however, there weren't many Western children where we were based, so we hung around with the kids who worked in the shacks on the beach selling things to tourists. Many were our age, some not even teenagers, and they were away from their parents who lived elsewhere in the country, often days away in remote, poor villages in the north. The children were sent south to the tourist areas to work and to send the money they made home. They slept in the beach shacks at night. They never complained and worked hard in the sun. They viewed it as an opportunity and an adventure. We were a curiosity to them as there were so few white children living in the area. Most of them spoke English and the ones that didn't communicated through the medium of cricket.

Often, richer Indian families would come to the beach from the cities for holidays and would want to play with us and hang out as it was deemed cool to be seen with Westerners. But they wouldn't want the local lads to play because of the class system. They were upper class and would tell the others to go away, but we'd insist and stick up for the poor kids. Their social system was so rigid that, rather than bend the rules and play together, they would storm off. They couldn't understand why rich Westerners would spend time with lowly beach workers. But the kids we met were real characters and much more fun.

Goa State Cricket Club was based nearby and Dad took Paul and me there to train with them. We were the only white kids on the team and although they were all friendly and welcoming, we were given the nickname 'White Monkeys'. It was racist abuse of sorts but there was no harm meant in it at all. When we told Dad, he said, 'Now you know what it's like for people on the other side of the world.'

Eventually, after a few months, we got bored with school and tried to explain to our parents that we were not learning anything useful. The home-schooling started again, but wasn't as rigidly enforced as the education authorities in the UK would have required. It was hard to concentrate when the beach and the sea were beckoning yards away.

Some things took a bit of getting used to. Time-keeping on public transport was adhered to with a huge degree of professional pride, but away from the railways things got done when they got done. Most people worked on 'Indian time'. You could go out for dinner and your meal would come out two hours later. We learned patience. The cities were, on the whole, frenetic, but once you journeyed away from them, the country settled into a much more laid-back pace of life.

Prices were often a mystery. You paid what you thought was a fair fee and never paid the first price quoted. Not many goods had price tags on them. We learned the art of negotiation and practised it ceaselessly. Prices varied wildly; you could go in one shop and pay one amount for bread and in the next shop the cost was triple. We learned the value of stuff. We also learned how to ask for things in the local language, Hindi, which had the effect of making people realize we were not tourists and lessened the chances of being charged inflated tourist rates.

When they felt confident enough that they knew the ropes and the way things operated in India, our parents organized our first trip out.

'We're going to Kerala,' Dad announced.

Kerala was a province a long train journey to the south of Goa. It was by the sea and a popular stop-off for travellers and holidaymakers. It had pristine beaches and a network of peaceful backwaters that irrigated swathes of paddy fields.

We took the overnight train and slept in the carriage with the locals. The trains were like micro-communities. People from all walks of life were crammed into them for the duration of the journey, some of which would last for days as the distances were so vast. I loved them. The carriages had bunk beds and everyone would chat through the night. Often we were the only white people on board and would immediately arouse curiosity.

'Why are you kids here, why are you not at school?' people would ask.

The train to Kerala was cramped and at parts of the route people would be hanging off it. In the daytime some would clamber on to the roof to keep cool. The toilet was a hole in the floor of the carriage and you'd have to do your business while the train travelled at 80mph, swaying violently around the bends. Bladder control was another useful skill I learned.

At stops a small army of hawkers would climb aboard to sell food and drink and at regular intervals young boys would walk down the carriages selling chai. We found that trains were the best way to travel. The views were unreal, like in the movie *Slumdog Millionaire*. It was sociable and fun and as was customary, when everyone woke up in the morning, they'd cough up phlegm loudly.

We arrived in the Keralan capital, Thiruvananthapuram, and found a driver to take us to a beach resort. From the guidebooks we had an idea where we wanted to stay, but hadn't booked ahead as our parents preferred to look at the accommodation on offer first. Throughout our travels they always tried to ensure they stayed in places that were family friendly. Some of the traveller hostels were a bit too lively for young children. Instead we tended to stay in hotels, guest houses, hill stations and villas. They cost a little more but, in comparison with UK prices, were still remarkably cheap.

Kerala was awesome: the sun-kissed beaches, the coconut-laden palms. It was a postcard come to life. We spent several weeks there and explored some days, then messed around on the beach on others. The backwaters were a highlight. The interconnected lakes, canals and rivers extended for almost half the length of the state. In parts it was like being in the Amazon rainforest, in others the American Bayou. There were towns and villages dotted around and many of them were geared for tourists. You could rent traditional-style houseboats which cruised the waterways or stay in shacks on stilts above the water.

The trip was the first of many. Sometimes we would travel by train, sometimes we would hire a driver. We became increasingly adventurous and went further afield.

The four-month deadline was rarely spoken about and, when it passed, it was obvious we were not going back anytime soon. There was simply too much to see and we'd hardly made a dent.

By the time we did eventually get back to the UK, it was the summer and we'd been away for six months. I think our parents would have preferred to stay in India longer still, but they wanted to get back to see Jo and Marie and to catch up with friends and family. We left everything in the villa. We had no home in the UK so we stayed in a holiday park in the New Forest. We had a large static home there, big enough for everyone. The site had a pool, leisure facilities, restaurants, football pitches and tennis courts.

It wasn't tropical paradise but for us kids it was ideal. We had been used to constant stimulation and we needed to be in a place where there were plenty of activities. The plan was always to go back to India. The villa was rented long-term and all our stuff was there. But we knew we were going to be in the UK for several months and joined the local cricket club. It was also good to be around Western children again and we made plenty of friends. There were always other children around to play with. Some found it hard to understand our living arrangements and their parents thought we were bonkers.

'You live where?'

'We live in India. We come from Croydon and we're staying here in a caravan for a few months,' I'd explain.

We'd gone from a nice middle-class house in Purley, then we went travelling to India, now we were in a static home. It was quite an unusual trajectory.

Some of the kids would laugh at us.

'You live in a caravan!' But it didn't bother me and Dad and Mum would just tell us not to let it bother us.

'Think about the kids we met travelling. Look how lucky you are in relation to them. Give it another couple of months and you'll be back on the beach playing cricket and travelling around,' they'd say.

It was around that time that I got the nickname Indy, partly because of the India connection and party because of Indiana Jones.

When the summer came to an end, our parents decided to invest long-term in their own caravan on the site so we would have a base for when we came back to the UK. They missed Jo and Marie and wanted somewhere familiar and permanent that we could return to.

Once again we said goodbye to the UK and headed back to the other side of the world, where we continued our global education.

We soon embarked on another journey and took the long train journey to Rajasthan in the north of the country. It is the largest province in India, roughly the size of Germany. Much of it is desert wilderness, but it is beautiful. In the capital, Jaipur, many of the buildings are made from blush-coloured masonry and when the dust hangs in the air at sunset, the whole city seems to glow a dusky pink colour.

We nearly didn't get there. The journey involved taking train connections, one of which was in the early hours of the morning. We had to disembark from one train and catch another. As we pulled into the connecting station, which was in a remote town in the middle of nowhere, we started to bundle off the train when Mattie called out, 'I've left my inhaler in the carriage.'

Rajasthan is known to be dusty and Mattie's inhaler was possibly the most important possession we had.

'I'll go and get it,' offered Paul. He turned around and walked back up the carriage as the rest of us climbed down the steps onto the platform to wait for him.

But after just a few seconds we heard the diesel engine of the train begin to rev and slowly the carriages began to inch forward.

'Paul!' Mum screamed.

My stomach lurched. After the station we were standing at, the train wasn't due to stop for a day. We saw Paul through the window of the carriage. We shouted at him. There was a look of panic on his face and he was running down the aisle with his backpack slung over his shoulders. The train moved faster and we left our bags where they were and started to jog alongside it.

'Run, Paul,' Dad called. 'Get off the bloody train.'

My brother emerged at the door. Mum was calling down the platform trying to get someone to stop the train. I trotted along by the door.

'Paul, throw your bag down,' I shouted. The train was picking up speed, belching diesel fumes into the night air. If he jumped with his bag on his back, he would hurt himself.

Paul did as he was told. I dodged the bag as it flew over my head. It was followed by my brother, who leaped free and landed just as we ran out of platform.

The rest of the journey was uneventful and Rajasthan ended up being one of Paul's favourite places in India. It was dry, hot and exotic with fascinating temples, mosques and markets. The people were very different from those in the south. One of the main ethnic groups was the Rajasthani gypsies. They wore stunning, colourful clothing with shiny metal sewn into it and were bedecked in jewels with big earrings. With their intricate ethnic tattoos and piercing green or blue eyes, they looked otherworldly.

In some places we visited we elicited a level of curiosity. We went far off the beaten track and ended up in some towns where people had never seen Westerners, apart from in magazines or on television. We went to one city, Belgan, which has a population the size of London, the huge majority of whom spoke English but had never seen white people. When they saw us, people there went out of their way to go and buy disposable cameras so they could take photographs. Mothers asked us to hold their babies for good luck. Grown men were fascinated. They had never seen Western clothing before. They would be engrossed by the polyester of our sports shorts, as if we were wearing garments from the future. Dad's mobile phone usually caused a stir because it had a colour screen and polyphonic ringtones. To an Indian at the time, it looked like something from the space age, and he delighted in giving demonstrations of it.

We saw amazing sights and scenery. I recall one boat trip across a bay in Goa. In the hills on one side of the curved natural harbour someone had built a huge, modern mansion complete with floor-to-ceiling glass walls and a helipad. The property wouldn't have looked out of place doubling as a villain's lair in a James Bond movie. On the other side of the bay, facing the millionaire mansion, there was a prison. It was dilapidated, old and grim. As the boat drew closer, I could see the arms of prisoners hanging through the bars on the windows. The two sights succinctly summed up the contradictions that visitors faced in the country.

We celebrated Diwali, the festival of lights, and spent our first Christmas in the villa and ate dinner on the beach, then went for a swim. In spring we took part in the Holi celebrations, a crazy free-for-all carnival of colour where participants pelt each other with dry powder paint and coloured water. Anyone and everyone was fair game and the fun took place in the streets, parks, and outside temples and buildings. In June the monsoon season started. I enjoyed it because it was cooler and quiet. The rain came down in sheets and made rivers of the streets. It was warm, like standing under a shower. It was beautiful. The beach shacks shut up. Our friends returned to their families and the resort became a ghost town. Sometimes I'd sit under shelter and draw. There was a different vibe. It was peaceful.

We knew the town inside out. We had bikes but mainly we'd walk. The weather was good and the pace of life became so laid-back, a stroll across town to get a fruit juice would take several hours. We'd stop and chat to people on the way, or perhaps have a game of cricket or football. It was a day out. I'd go off exploring and meet people. We had more time. We had to amuse ourselves, and because we were with each other a lot, we would end up going off and doing things independently for some time away from everyone else.

We spent a lot of time with our parents. They weren't working so we did a lot of activities together. Some days we'd play chess or read newspapers to keep up to date with what was going on in the world.

Inevitably the trip got extended again. In fact, it was no longer a trip; it was life. We got a longer visa and although we still returned to the UK, the visits home became longer apart; once a year or every eighteen months.

When we did go back, family noticed a change. We looked different. We were all thin, healthy and more chilled-out. I was mistaken for an Indian several times. We spoke differently, too. In India, to make yourself understood, it was important to nod your head, speak in an Indian accent and wave your fingers like the locals did. It sounds bizarre but it worked. The problem was we did it so much in India, when we came back to the UK we still did it and had to remember to stop, in case it looked like we were taking the mickey. Dad was the worst offender. We'd pull him up on it and remind him he was in the UK.

We grew up. Our priorities changed. Little things stopped bothering us. In the grand scheme of things we realized it wasn't worth worrying about the small stuff. If people were hassling us we wouldn't be too bothered. We were more stoic. At home our friends were preoccupied with the latest gadgets or what toys they were getting for Christmas. They had their priorities the wrong way round.

CHAPTER 5

Sea, Sand, Snakes and Mosquitoes

THE SEA FOR years was the first thing I heard in the morning and the last thing I heard at night. Unconsciously I knew its moods and rhythms. In the mornings I would lie awake and listen to what it was saying. I knew just by listening whether it was a day for swimming or a day when the waves and undertow would be too strong.

'It is powerful, kids, respect it,' our parents had cautioned early in our journey. 'No matter what else happens, Mother Nature is the one thing that can change in an instant and flip your world around. Nature is the most powerful thing there is.'

Dad had been pulled under before and we'd seen a few of the beach kids get in trouble too. In the bay where we stayed there were undercurrents that would pull you out if the tide was particularly strong and we learned an important lesson. Go with the current, don't fight against it.

I loved the waves. They could be ferocious some days and then I'd avoid them, but when conditions were right the swells would be big enough to body surf. I'd launch onto an inbound wave and let it carry me on its crest and then give into it as it broke over my body. I'd float motionless, my body relaxed as the sea dragged me under, tumbled me around and then sent me back to the surface, like a cat playing with a mouse.

The sea was untamed but I could read it. I knew the ebb and flow of the tides. I learned to look at the phases of the moon and from them I'd know what tides to expect. I knew the best places to swim depending on the weather conditions. I knew our beach like the back of my hand.

After several years away from the UK, we were all strong swimmers. When we weren't off on our travels, life revolved around the sea. It was our lounge, our playroom and our garden.

I was fifteen when I plucked the old man from the ocean.

I was on the beach. The sun was up, there was a breeze and I could tell by the size, shape and sound of the waves that the undercurrents would be strong in certain areas of the bay. I watched the man and his wife as they swam into view. They were a long way out. The waves crashed on the shore a few feet in front of me. There was nothing obvious to suggest danger, but I sensed enough to keep watch on them. They were an elderly Indian couple. I could tell by their easy swimming technique that they were regular swimmers. They glided effortlessly. The parts of their bodies above the surface, their heads and shoulders, hardly moved and they created hardly any splashes: the sign of a good swimmer.

I was with Mum, she watched them too.

At a point, about fifty yards out from shore, I could see a change in the man's technique. His strokes quickened. He was splashing. He was struggling. I sat up and watched intently. The lady he was with was struggling too and I could see she was being carried in an arc by a current away from him. The man had stopped swimming and instead was waving. He was being pulled under. The sound of his calls for help drifted into the shore.

The adrenaline hit me like a bolt and without thinking I jumped up and ran into the water. I didn't hear Mum calling me back. Several yards in front of me I saw the man go under. By the time I reached him, he had resurfaced but was limp. I could feel the current tugging me and I grabbed him, tried to pull his head above the water line and concentrated on keeping us at the surface.

I didn't fight the undertow and instead swam with it at an angle to the shore. Ahead of us I saw the lady who had been with the man stagger onto the sand safely and look over at us, concern etched in her face. I felt the sand of the shore underfoot and dragged the unconscious man out of the water. Mum ran over. She was trained in first aid and laid the man down and began administering CPR. I knelt by the side of her, panting and shaking.

After a tense minute, the man spluttered back to life. We stayed with him while one of the beach kids ran to get a local medic who came and took over.

I thought I'd been a hero but, later that evening, Mum gave me a ticking-off.

'What do you think you were doing, rushing out into the water without a thought about how dangerous it was?'

'But . . .' I stammered.

'Don't ever put yourself at risk like that again,' she concluded.

Lots of things in India were risky. Driving was particularly dangerous. Dad never did. He always left it to drivers. We'd take cabs, rickshaws and tuk-tuks, cycle or walk. For longer journeys we would take the train or hire a driver and vehicle.

Snakes were a constant consideration. We had several close encounters. In the heat of the day you would often find them curled up in out-of-the-way places. They were shy by nature and would get out the way if they knew you were coming, but if you startled one you could find yourself in trouble. We learned that the best way to ensure the snakes knew where you were was through noise and vibration. It became a habit to walk with a stick and tap the ground, especially at night. The vibrations would warn the snakes, which would, in turn, slither away.

I played football with a local side and there was a shortcut to the ground through a paddy field. These marshy areas were favourite hiding places for snakes and this particular field was known for cobras so, whenever I walked through it, I would clap my hands and shout. If we got home late at night, we would clap and stamp our feet as we walked through the front door.

We had a few close encounters. Rosie was running through the grounds of the resort one afternoon and jumped off a step. She landed inches from a snake that was coiled on the path. A waiter saw it recoil and slither away. He told her later that it was definitely a venomous one.

Once, when I was playing football with a few of the local lads on a patch of dusty wasteland, I disturbed a sand snake which had buried itself below the surface. It sprang at me and I managed to jump over it before it could sink its fangs into my leg. On a few occasions I'd be out walking somewhere and happen upon a mongoose fighting a cobra.

Our closest encounter happened in the lounge. We were alerted by Rosie's screams. She'd seen a black snake slither across the room and hide under the sofa. Very quietly and gingerly, Dad gestured to Paul and I to move the sofa out the way while he stood at the side with a cricket bat raised and ready to strike. On the count of three we shifted the furniture and Dad lunged forward and smashed the poor animal over the head. He gave it several more whacks just to make sure; you couldn't be too careful. Mum taught us that if any of us were bitten, the others would have to suck out the poison and spit it out. The thought of that alone made us extra careful.

While snakes were something to look out for and avoid, the real danger, according to waiters and people who worked on the beaches, were coconuts. They could be deadly and apparently killed more people a year in Goa than snakes did. Certainly, if one dropped on your head you would know about it. They weighed a couple of kilos each, were rock hard and grew up to sixty feet from the ground. They regularly went through roofs, crashing through tiles and many coconut-bearing palm trees had safety nets around them to keep whoever and whatever was underneath them safe. The municipal services would regularly send people up the trees to cut down the potentially deadly fruit before it got too ripe and fell of its own accord.

One missed Dad by inches when he walked under a tree early in our travels. It landed in the sand next to him with a loud THWUMP! We avoided walking under palms after that.

Other notably dangerous fruit were watermelons; mainly because they could give you a bad case of the runs. They absorb water and watermelon hawkers left them in the river to keep cool; the same river people used as a toilet. Hygiene standards took a bit of getting used to. We became blasé about seeing rats near restaurants and learned not to look in the kitchens of the places we ate in. It wasn't worth it. If you did you would never eat out again.

Malaria was also a consideration. The air around paddy fields would become thick with mosquitoes at dusk and, to begin with, we took anti-malarial tablets but that didn't work out too well. We'd heard that they could make you ill if you took them for too long so, in the end, we gave up and discovered the local solution: a product called Odomos. Everyone used it for their children and it was held in high regard. It was as important in Indian homes as soap. It smelled of lemons and we coated ourselves in it. Every day, as soon as the sun started to set, the call would go up in the villa.

'Where's the Odomos?'

We bought bottles of the stuff because there were so many of us. The man who owned our local store would place a bottle on the counter as soon as one of us walked in. It was incredibly effective. None of us ever got bitten.

Despite what you might sometimes hear, if you were careful and sensible, India was a safe place. We were allowed freedoms there that our peers back in the UK would never have dreamed of. It was safe to walk around on your own. The only thing we ever had stolen was a football shirt. Mattie left it on the beach and wandered off to do something. When he returned, it had gone. A week later, we saw one of the local kids wearing it and accused him of taking it. He denied everything and said it was his; why a local in Goa would be wearing a QPR shirt was anyone's guess, but we left it anyway. There were more important things to worry about in life than a stolen T-shirt.

There was no traffic to worry about in the resort and we had the luxury of being allowed to play, take risks and learn by our own errors. Our parents were always careful and mitigated risks. If we went to a festival or to a busy market, there would always be a pre-arranged meeting point to get back to in case anyone got lost and we researched new towns before we went. Mum and Dad always ensured we went to places appropriate for families. We were taught to be careful of pickpockets and were always encouraged to think of personal safety.

Back home my friends would have been shut in classrooms or playing in the dreary local park, protected by the soft rubber matting. In India we had the whole town and beach as our playground and a procession of colourful and interesting characters to interact with. I strongly believe that we all learned and gained more in terms of knowledge and life skills in the years we spent travelling than we ever would have at school in the suburbs.

The only time we ever really had a drama was when Mattie suffered a particularly bad asthma attack. He'd had them all the time back in the UK but in India he only ever had a few. Still, it was very scary.

We had oxygen for Mattie and a nebulizer that he used. Whenever we returned to the UK we would stock up on medication to take back with us. My parents also tried him with ayurvedic medicine: a form of natural, alternative medicine that is widely used in India and given in the health service there. In brief, the technique works by balancing different aspects of the body.

Mattie's attack happened during monsoon season. It was not sudden. He got progressively worse over a number of days. It was particularly humid that year and Mattie was sensitive to changes in the weather. At his worst he was pale and went blue in the lips and said his heart was hurting as he struggled to take shallow breaths. It was frightening. The local doctor came and sat with him all night. Mum and Dad were incredibly stressed and feared that the attack would get the better of him. He was hooked up to a nebulizer but nothing was working. After four days he eventually stabilized and we decided to go back to the UK for a while so he could get his strength back. It shook us all up, and afterwards our parents cancelled the alternative medicine, fearing Mattie had suffered a reaction to it.

The Indians we met were very resourceful. There was no social security system there, so you either worked or you went hungry. There were few big employers. People worked for themselves and set up their own businesses: shops, stalls, services and trades. It was a nation of entrepreneurs and that spirit suited us fine. There were plenty of opportunities to make money.

I would go off to the market and sell stuff that I brought over from the UK. Sportswear and football shirts were particularly sought after. I could buy cheap football shirts from markets in the UK and sell them at a profit to rich Indians on holiday in Goa who believed they were authentic clubwear because I was a Westerner. Using some of the money I made, I bought cheap DVDs and then took them back to the UK where I sold them at a profit. It was an international business. I was thirteen when I started it. There was always trading and bartering. We traded with anyone: Western tourists, rich Indians, Tibetans who had come to Goa to work.

In town there were loads of jewellery shops selling cheap gold and gems to tourists and Paul became friends with one of the owners, a man named Jeedi, and began to spend a lot of time with him learning about the precious metal and gem trade. It was like an apprenticeship. Paul soon learned about the different types of stones, how much they were worth wholesale, how to tell if they were genuine and how much people would pay for them. Paul sat with Jeedi all day in his shop and went to the factory where he had his stock made as well. It was mutually beneficial because while Paul learned a trade, the jeweller had a Westerner in his shop which meant that tourists tended to trust him more and wouldn't be scared to go in and browse.

Although Dad was in what he termed as semi-retirement, the hiatus didn't last long. He was a natural businessman and always on the look-out for an opportunity. Increasingly he had become interested in the Internet and the possibilities it held. The dot com bubble had burst, but India was still a place where the Internet was growing and there were plenty of opportunities. Dad wanted to piggyback on the popularity of the technology. He was an early adopter. His mobile phone was a conversation piece in some of the less developed places we happened upon and he also had a laptop. He was probably one of the first people in India to have a 3G connection, which at the time would have been hugely expensive. It was the days before dongles and his laptop had a built-in modem card.

Dad came up with the idea of developing an online monitoring system that parents could use to keep track of their children's school achievements; specifically in regards to sport. It was called Sports Recognition. Parents would be able to log on to a secure site which would be updated regularly by the school. They would be able to monitor their children's progress and whether they had attended certain classes and clubs. For busy parents it was a way of keeping up to date with their child's progress. They wouldn't have to wait until parents' evening. Dad's plan was to sell the software to schools and government departments.

He found programmers in India who worked with him developing the idea and by 2004 it was almost ready to go live. It looked good and worked well. It had been tested for glitches and we already had the contacts in the education market from the days of Rose Fashions. Dad planned to have me, and eventually Paul, work on it with him. Sadly, Dad's idea never came to commercial fruition but it is testament to his foresight that, today, many schools and parents use a similar system.

Over the years we built up an exotic network of friends. At one point Dad 'adopted' a young Irish man named Ian. He'd travelled to India to see his sister and decided to stay. They got on well and he'd often come round to the house and watch football. Paul was friends with Jeedi the jeweller and we were also pals with the hotel manager, Rudi, who was half Goan and half Portuguese and liked a drink. Paul and I had friends our own age but they were transitory; the beach kids would move on eventually, as would Western families on holiday, so mainly we hung out with adults. We played pool in a nearby hotel but we never went to the busy backpacker bars.

We spent a lot of time together and became very close. We worked together and played together. We ate together as a family in the evenings and after dinner would play chess or cards. We spent a lot of time chilling out with each other. We probably knew our parents better than most kids did because we were not in the usual domestic routine. Life was relaxing and we saw another side of them as they were relaxed too. The four years we spent travelling were remarkable. By breaking away from convention, our parents had changed us in ways we never realized until tragedy struck.

CHAPTER 6

Bridging the Poverty Gap

IN INDIA WE were never encouraged to shy away from one of the fundamental facts of life in the country we'd chosen to make our home: that vast swathes of its population were terribly poor and disadvantaged. While many families would rock up to Goa on a two-week package tour and avoid the poverty, we never did. I never got the chance to ask Mum and Dad whether they had a plan; whether they knew that exposing us to the difficulties and cruelties life can present would allow us to develop a maturity and resilience beyond our years. Whether they did or not, the school-of-life education we received by being taken out of mainstream school was a gift which eventually saved our lives.

Learning about the harsh realities of life in the developing world was a hard lesson but a necessary one. Poverty and human misery were not always apparent, but they were there, chipping away at your conscience. If you were so inclined, you could turn your head. You could eat at the Western restaurants, stay at the best-rated hotels, shop in the air-conditioned stores and take taxis to bypass the deprivation you faced on foot. You could cross the road to avoid beggars; you could try hard not to think about the staff in the back of the inhumane, furnace-hot kitchens working for a few pounds a week. You could ignore the crippled, elderly gardener on his knees cutting grass with scissors in forty-degree heat and you could convince yourself that the children with dirt-smeared faces in rags on the streets in the darkness were not homeless. But if you had anything resembling a heart, you would look the poverty in the eye and you'd be rightly shocked. For me, over time that initial shock subsided but, when it did, it was replaced by a sense of purpose and a desire to try and do something to help, no matter how small.

It was the same with our parents. When I first got to India at the age of thirteen, I didn't know what the term 'social conscience' meant, but they had one. Rose Fashions had been about distributing money and helping charities and schools help themselves and they had taken pains to make us aware of how lucky we were on a global scale. I knew I was better off than many kids in the world. I had a family who loved me. I had food, shelter and clothes. Before I got to India I'd never witnessed real poverty and, when I did, it was unsettling. Mum and Dad did not try and shield us from the harsh realities of life in a poor country. Ignorance isn't always bliss and they saw it as part of the experience; there was no point looking the other way. If we did, we wouldn't be true to ourselves and we would learn nothing and take nothing away.

As we knew from our very first holiday in India, when we visited the children's home, there were charities operating in the town raising awareness of the issues poverty created and collecting money to fund projects. One of these charities that was active locally was a charitable trust, which ran a number of projects to help street children: kids who had been orphaned, abandoned by their parents or who were so neglected and abused at home, they ran away. The charity ran a school, shelters and four children's homes in Goa and other provinces. It had volunteers who would talk to tourists and invite them along to a home it ran for orphans in the town. They had a vehicle and would happily drive people to the homes for a visit.

One of the charity's philosophies was that it gave the children in its care a hand up, not a hand out. It provided children with an education in addition to shelter and food.

Our parents got involved after speaking to a volunteer who was manning the charity's stall in one of the local markets. They had never been the type of people who could turn away and, when they heard about the charity, they wanted to see what they could do to help. They went for a visit to one of the homes and they took us along.

There were around thirty children living there: boys and girls of different ages, ranging from around three or four to teenagers. The house was small for so many kids, but clean. The boys slept in one big room and the girls slept in another. There weren't beds for everyone, instead they had bedding rolls. There was a small kitchen in which volunteers prepared three meals a day, and a dining room with a single table. There was also a classroom and bathroom. At the front there was a yard with sand and dirt in which the children could play. It was basic, but you could tell the children liked being there. I noticed that all of them were barefoot as they played on the equipment in the yard.

They were excited to see Westerners and crowded round us as we were shown around. We got drawn into a game of cricket and, while some spoke English, communication wasn't a problem. They just wanted to play.

The visit didn't last long, but it sowed a seed in our parents. They decided afterwards that they would help as volunteers and they volunteered us as well, reasoning that as we were not at school, we should be doing something constructive and helpful with our time. We didn't complain. It wasn't really like work. We just went along and hung out with the kids.

That was how our link with the orphans of India began: with our parents' desire to put something back and to try and make a difference in some way.

We became regular visitors to the home. We helped dish out the food, we played cricket and football with the kids, chatted and socialized with them.

We also helped man the stall in the market and we would go there and encourage other tourists to sign up and make donations. As with Paul and his jewellery job, the charity realized that it helped having Westerners on board because other Westerners were more likely to stop and talk and to trust us. We encouraged others to visit the home and volunteer.

The children in the home were there for a variety of different reasons. Some of them had recently been orphaned in the Gujarat earthquake: a natural disaster which claimed 20,000 lives and destroyed 400,000 homes. The kids were still living with the trauma of having lost their families. Grief affected them in different ways. They were normal and playful but, every so often, would become withdrawn and sad.

Others were there because their families had abandoned them, while others were victims of abuse. There were a lot of children who were placed in the home for their own safety because their parents had alcohol problems. Some were victims of sexual abuse. One boy had been sexually abused by his own dad. Others had been beaten.

Many of them were happy to be where they were. Conditions were poor and cramped, but they were safe and cared for. They were affectionate and you could tell they craved affection and security. The ones who had just arrived were inevitably distressed and uncomfortable and it was our job to play with them and just allow them to be children again. It was upsetting to hear their stories and a few were so horrific they were hard to believe.

One boy was twelve years old and only had one arm.

He told his story to Paul.

'My parents held me down on a railway track until the train went over me,' he explained.

Paul shuddered.

'Why?'

'For begging,' the boy replied. 'Better money.'

Horrifically maimed children were worth more as beggars. They elicited more sympathy and more money. Sadly, the boy's story was not unique. We met another child who'd had acid thrown in his face and was blinded in one eye for the same reason. His wounds would earn him more money.

The children in that home taught us more about resilience and determination than we would have learned at school. They were some of the most disadvantaged people on the planet, yet they still managed to remain positive and hopeful of the future. They valued what little they had and they valued the opportunity they had been given to have security and an education. They looked forward in hope, rather than backwards in bitterness. They'd been knocked down by life but had got back up and got on with the business of living. Most of the kids we met accepted what had happened to them and moved on. They were happier than a lot of the wealthy people we knew back in the UK. They realized happiness was not about money or material things, it was about having your head in the right place.

The tourist traps of Goa attracted beggars, drawn by the lure of Western money, and also migrant workers who were paid little and lived in slums. Their presence was bad for the image India wanted to portray to the rest of the world: that of a burgeoning successful developing nation and, as tourism picked up in the province, the slums were moved. Tourist guides wouldn't take you to them, but you could find them if you looked. The charity also did outreach work in the slum areas on the outskirts of town. We went there with our parents and other volunteers. It was a sprawling shanty town with open sewers carved in the baked earth which ran between shacks made of corrugated iron, loading pallets and polythene sheets. Whole families lived in them. Others lived under clumsily made frames with black plastic bin liners stretched over them to keep the monsoon rains out. Children splashed barefoot through the filthy water. The smell was stomach-churning.

The first time we visited was scary. We went with a supply of pens for the children. As we walked through the first alleys, more and more children came out, realizing that we were Westerners with gifts. There were no manners or patient queues. One kid reached into the box I was holding, grabbed a handful and ran away. I had the advantage of being taller than the children and held the box over my head, which solved the problem of over-eager hands. However, soon the adults arrived and started grabbing as well. There was some jostling and some stern words from Mum and Dad and the other volunteers before the situation calmed down. It was understandable. Pens were coveted currency. They could be sold for a few rupees which, in turn, could buy a meal for a family or alcohol to help someone forget the miserable situation they were in.

After the shock of that first visit, we went back several times. We got rickshaws to the slums and distributed pens and paper. We would accompany local nurses who set up visiting clinics and helped with inoculations. We would check and clean minor cuts and injuries, applying disinfectant and plasters. We got to know a lot of the children living there. We took them fruit and food, played football or cricket with them, entertained them, and gave them pencils, books or drawing paper. It wasn't like working. It was more like playing. Our parents didn't do it through pity and they didn't do it because they felt we needed to be taught a lesson or because they felt we were spoilt in any way. They just felt it was the right thing to do and they wanted us to see how children lived in other parts of the world. They never made us do anything we didn't want to do and, more often than not, we enjoyed getting involved. Sometimes it was uncomfortable, such as when we were with kids with polio or leprosy, but it was also very fulfilling. The kids didn't want pity, they didn't want people to feel sorry for them. They needed a bit of help and we were happy to give it.

Without realizing it, the work we did in the slums changed our perspectives on life. For example, Paul and I used to moan about sharing a room when we lived in our house in Purley. We realized how petty that was when we'd visit a family of eight who were all living in one room under a tarpaulin roof. We learned to be thankful for the small things in life. When you saw kids go mad over colouring pens, you began to realize that having the latest games console or the latest phone was meaningless in the general scheme of things. In the slums, an orange could make the difference between someone having a good day and a bad day. If you gave a kid an orange, they would be overjoyed. Give a kid an orange in the UK and they might chuck it back at you and ask for sweets. In the UK my peers would be fussing over clothes and the latest fashions. In the Goan slum, kids would be in ragged T-shirts with no shoes. If they cut themselves or injured themselves, they got on with it. Each time we returned to the New Forest for our regular visits, I saw the world with new eyes and became increasingly aware of the gap between the haves and the have-nots.

In India there was no shortage of underprivileged people to help and rather than ignore the poverty, we became adept at spotting it. After a while I could spot a neglected child or a homeless one. The old lonely people made me sad. Indians had big families so they'd have children to look after them when they aged. Every old beggar told a sad story; perhaps their children had died. Sometimes I would see someone on the road, slumped, and wonder whether they were dead or alive. There were some places we went to and realized that a situation wasn't repairable; all you could do was your best. Even now we know that we can't change the world, we can't save everyone, but we do what we can and hopefully we might inspire more people to do something. You can't fix it all.

At the beginning of 2004 we returned to the UK. We'd been travelling for four years and had had some amazing adventures and seen some incredible sights. Dad's website was almost ready to go live and our parents felt it was time to start thinking about the next phase of their lives. I suspect the money might have been running low too.

They'd started to think about either settling in other destinations or back in the UK. Australia and New Zealand were mentioned. The prospect of school also reared its ugly head. I was sixteen and hadn't been in full-time education for many years; neither had Paul, Mattie or Rosie. In terms of maturity, we were all far more advanced than any kids we knew, but Mum and Dad still felt it was important we had some qualifications so we moved back into the caravan and I enrolled at Brockenhurst College where I did a vocational course and a GCSE in English.

I didn't mind going back and made some very good friends there. For his part, Paul hated school and failed the exams he eventually took. The sum total of our educational achievement was a B Tech in sports and a grade C in English GCSE.

In the summer, while it was still being decided what we were going to do, I took a job in a leisure centre near Bournemouth on the south coast. I trained as a lifeguard and passed with flying colours. I spent the days by the pool; I made plenty of friends and got to chat to plenty of cute girls who were out of my league. Mattie and Rosie also went to a local school. For Paul and me it was probably too late to catch up, but they still had a chance of academic success.

It was a fun summer. We caught up with friends and family we hadn't seen for a long time and spent a lot of time with our sisters, Jo and Marie. Marie was planning to marry her partner, Liam, the following year and Mum had been increasingly involved in the wedding plans. It was going to be a big church affair and Mum was making the bridesmaid dresses. Marie had travelled to India on several occasions to talk through arrangements. Proud Dad was looking forward to walking her down the aisle. Liam was a great guy, loyal and dependable, and Dad liked him immensely.

Towards the end of the summer, Mum and Dad began to talk about going back to India. We still had our base there. The plan was to go one last time and tie up loose ends. Dad had final tweaks to make to the website with the developers he was working with, and Jo was going to come over for a holiday as well.

Our parents also liked the idea of seeing another destination while we were on that side of the world. Our travels had taken us all over India but, apart from our stop in Jordan and a few weeks we'd spent in Cyprus in 2002, we had not been away from the subcontinent. We started to think about travelling to see somewhere else. I got the impression it would be a last hurrah before we settled back down again; a holiday within the big holiday.

A few years previously, when we'd spent a couple of months in Kerala, we'd met a man named Baba who we became friendly with. He owned a beach shack and he'd come to the hotel where we stayed in the evenings for something to eat and drink. He'd sit and chat to us. He was Sri Lankan and he told us all about his homeland. Like most Sri Lankan men he was obsessed with cricket so we had a lot in common. He knew Russell Arnold, a hugely popular Sri Lankan batsman, and would always drop his name in the conversation, causing me, Paul and Dad to look at each other with raised eyebrows. Baba recommended Sri Lanka as a destination. He described the beaches, the friendly people and the stunning scenery. It sounded like a cool place. We'd read about it in some of the guidebooks that travellers had left around the hotel in Goa and in some of the places we stayed in India. When you speak to travellers you realize that there are certain routes they take and Sri Lanka was on many of their itineraries.

So Dad went out and bought the Lonely Planet guide to Sri Lanka one day and sat down with us in the evening and asked what we thought. There was surfing there, there were unspoilt beaches, it was big enough to explore over several weeks; it sounded ideal. Paul mentioned that he had a Sri Lankan friend from Croydon and would quite like to go so he could tell his mate he'd been there. I thought it would make another interesting stamp on my passport. Mattie and Rosie were happy as it meant their assimilation back in the UK school system was postponed. Jo was happy to come along too, so we started making plans. We would fly back to India, spend some time there, then hop on a jet to Sri Lanka where we would spend Christmas 2004, explore the island for as long as we wanted or until we got bored, and then we'd come back to the UK in time for Marie's wedding.

CHAPTER 7

The Last Holiday

PAUL AND I left India with our parents, Mattie, Rosie and Jo a week before Christmas in 2004 and flew into the Sri Lankan capital, Colombo. Paul had a strange feeling as we approached the island which he told me about after everything that happened. He explained that he'd felt uneasy on the plane and that the journey seemed different somehow, like something bigger was waiting for us when we touched down. As the plane approached, he looked at the sea and had a strange, uneasy feeling.

'It was the same feeling you get when you forget something,' he explained.

The island of Sri Lanka is a bit smaller than England, which meant there would be no long journeys to contend with and it was packed with lots to do and see. There were eight UNESCO World Heritage sites to visit. There were ruins, temples, forests and mountains. There were national parks where herds of elephants roamed. There were beaches where turtles stopped to lay their eggs and coves ideal for snorkelling and surfing.

Despite the wealth of activities and attractions packed into a relatively small area, Sri Lanka remained off the beaten track for less adventurous travellers. While there were plenty of hotels and hostels along the coast, it was still underdeveloped in comparison with other destinations. This was largely due to the civil war that was fought in the country between 1983 and 2009 between the government and a militant organization called the Tamil Tigers. The Tamils were an ethnic group without a homeland, spread around Asia. They made up around fifteen per cent of the Sri Lankan population and the Tamil Tigers fought an insurgency against government forces to try and create an independent Tamil state in the north and east of the island.

Sri Lanka suffered greatly in the conflict which caused significant hardships for the population, environment and the economy. Up to 100,000 people were killed in the fighting. The tactics used by the Tamil Tigers resulted in the organization being listed as a terrorist group by several international governments, including the United States, India, Canada and the EU. In return, the government forces were accused of human rights abuses and brutality against the Tamil minority.

The island certainly had its problems, but much of the conflict was confined to the more remote parts and in 2002 a ceasefire agreement was signed between the two sides after peace talks and international mediation.

Sri Lanka was a relatively peaceful place when we arrived there and as the dark shadow of war receded somewhat, the tourist industry began to develop. From the guides we read it was easy to see why. It was an island of beautiful, unspoilt beaches, timeless ruins, welcoming people, mouth-watering cuisine and cheap prices. You could surf on the beach in the morning and see elephants on a safari in the afternoon. In the cooler mountains there were lush forests to explore, verdant tea plantations to visit and spectacular train rides to take. Sri Lanka even laid claim to the world's oldest living tree. We knew it was going to be an action-packed, interesting trip.

Colombo Airport was much like the Indian airports we had visited but smaller. It was hectic but not chaotic. Every airport in the developing world appeared to be the same. They were all full of people drawn there hoping to make a fast buck from the newly arrived foreigners.

We made our way quickly out the front of the terminal to the taxi rank, politely declining the people who tried to help with our bags or lure us to their hotels and resorts. We had already chosen where we were going. The most popular beach resorts on the south-west of the teardrop-shaped island were Galle and Matara, but rather than stay in the built-up towns we decided to make our way slowly down the coast, staying in the less developed, more authentic, traditional villages.

We hired a driver with a small minibus after haggling a price, loaded our bags on board, piled in and headed straight out through the city. The journey out of town took us through streets filled with tuk-tuks and rickshaws. While some of the districts were modern and clean, others were colourful and ramshackle. Kiosks selling cigarettes, phonecards, sweets and general supplies lined the streets and traders piled fruit and vegetables on sheets to sell.

The highway to the south took us through the main commercial district, Galle Road, which was clean and modern. We headed out down the coast and soon the offices, apartments and shops melted away and were replaced by lush forest on one side and blue white-tipped ocean on the other.

An hour away from the city we found a quiet little village on a bay of golden sand. We'd read about some beach houses there which were available for rent and we asked the driver to stop so Mum and Dad could have a look. We were all tired and looking forward to relaxing and having a meal. The place was ideal. Like many of the tourist areas in Sri Lanka, the accommodation was right on the beach, where land was more valuable. There was a house big enough for us all and nearby restaurants and bars, but in a family-friendly location.

We booked in for a night. Our parents never initially paid for more than one night's accommodation when we went somewhere new in case there was a nightclub or building site next door that the guides had failed to mention.

We had a peaceful night's sleep and woke to glorious sunshine the following day. It was the start of the dry season, when temperatures hovered around the high twenties. I woke early as usual. I was sharing a room with Paul and he was still asleep. I got up. The house was quiet. Everyone else was still asleep or in their rooms. I enjoyed the mornings. I'd always been an early riser and it felt like the part of the day that belonged to me. As the rest of the family gradually woke, the noise levels would inevitably rise. I'd have to shout sometimes to be heard above the Forkan cacophony. But in the early morning everything was still and peaceful. The house was on one level and I walked out of the bedroom, quietly closing the door behind me so as not to wake anyone else, and through the main living area. Our bags were still packed. It was pointless unpacking them until we knew whether we were going to be staying where we were for any length of time. I reached into mine and pulled out a pair of swimming shorts which I changed into.

I opened the front door and sunlight streamed in. I blinked in the light until my eyes adjusted. Despite the early hour, it was already warm. The sound of exotic birds occasionally broke the silence. I could hear parrots. I smiled to myself. The beach, the sound of the waves, the sunshine, sand underfoot; four years ago it would have all seemed alien and exotic to me, but now it felt like home. I felt as comfortable arriving in a far-flung location as I did living in the New Forest in the UK. I felt no apprehension and, wherever I went, I felt the desire to explore.

I walked down the beach to the water's edge where the waves peacefully lapped at the shoreline. The village we were staying in was situated in a sheltered bay and so the waves were gentle. The sea was turquoise and clear. I paddled in. It was warm. I looked down and saw several tiny fish dart around between my legs. It's a good day for snorkelling, I thought to myself. We hadn't brought snorkelling gear with us, but on the way to our accommodation we'd seen plenty of tourist shops selling cheap beach equipment. We usually bought what we needed when we arrived at a location, then left it there for other children to use.

I dunked under the waves and kicked out from the shore for a swim. The water was calm and there were no undercurrents. After about twenty minutes I went back inside. Mum and Dad had woken up and were sitting at a table in the dining area discussing going to find a local shop to buy in some supplies for breakfast.

Christmas was a week away, but in Sri Lanka we couldn't have been further from the usual December madness of advertising and over-consumption. The few decorations and lights up in restaurants and hotels were there for the benefit of the tourists and the small Christian minority on the island. Knowing we would be there on Christmas Day, we had packed presents for each other but they were small.

We stayed where we were for a couple of days, relaxing on the beach, snorkelling and exploring the village before we packed up, hired another taxi and headed further down the coast. We spent a few more days at another, larger town, all the while drawing up a plan of action for the days and weeks ahead.

'We'll relax around the beaches until after Christmas. There's no point heading inland until after that,' explained Dad.

On 23 December, we headed further down the island to the town of Weligama, 30 kilometres from Galle. The name means Sandy Village and Weligama sat on the very southern curve of the Sri Lankan teardrop, exposed to the vastness of the Indian Ocean. While there were hotels and hostels along the bay on which the town was built, it was also a commercial fishing centre with a market where the day's catches were sold by the fishermen who lived there. It was a busy, thriving town connected to the rest of the country by the main coast road and a railway line, which also ran close to the seafront and served as a convenient footpath for pedestrians who didn't want to brave the traffic. The focal point in the busy town was the four-storey mosque, which was topped by a large green dome. The narrow streets were lined with stalls and shacks selling everything from fruit and fish – which was filleted and gutted in the open on dirty wooden blocks – to brightly coloured sarongs, which many of the men wore. The soundtrack was the usual buzz of old cars, motorbikes, tuk-tuks, bicycles and the occasional blare of traditional music. Open drains ran down most of the streets. In the middle of the bay there was a tiny island known as Taprobane on which a small house had been built. It had belonged to a writer who used it as a retreat. When the tide was out, it was possible to walk across and explore.

The town was famous for its stilt fishermen whose traditional, unique style of fishing involved perching on poles dug into the sea bed and casting their lines out to sea. It was also known for surfing. A reef offshore acted as a break for the waves and ensured there were good conditions most of the year. It was an ideal place for beginners to learn when the sea was calm and there was a surfers' hostel on the beach. We stayed in a place called Neptune Resort, a few yards along from the hostel. It was situated directly on the beach and was away from the town centre.

The accommodation consisted of a small central hotel, several bungalows and two-storey, hexagonal pagoda-type buildings painted bright white and blue, all set in manicured gardens. Many of the rooms faced directly onto the beach. The Neptune was owned by a friendly Italian couple and the clientele was a mix of nationalities, mainly European, with several Italians and a German couple who had a young child. It was comfortable, family-friendly, clean and well equipped, with an open-air bar and restaurant area.

We stayed in the bungalows. Paul and I shared one, Mum and Dad stayed with Mattie and Rosie in another and Jo had her own room. She was due to stay with us for Christmas Day, then leave in the evening and head back to the UK. Mum and Dad's bungalow was on the beachfront facing the sea, ours was one row back, around 30 metres from them and facing inland.

On our first night we were sitting in the restaurant after dinner and got talking to a young Canadian guy who was there with his family. He noticed we were playing cards and brought over a game to show us. It was Risk, a board game where players take control of armies and the object is global domination. We'd never played it before and the man taught us the rules. Paul and I loved it and played it repeatedly for the rest of the night.

On Christmas Eve we went exploring in the town and spent the afternoon on the beach. Half of it was choppy where the reef created a break and the other half was calm, clear and ideal for snorkelling.

There was a definite Christmas vibe in the hotel, with a tree in the restaurant and decorations, mainly because the owners were Catholics and because most of the guests were Westerners. Even in India, the places where we'd previously spent Christmas had got into the spirit of the season and put up trees and decorations. Turkey was hard to come by, however, and most years we'd had chicken or fish. One year in India we had barbecued shark.

Our folks would always get us presents, but they were small gifts and usually practical things. We didn't buy a lot of stuff and we didn't have Christmas lists or write to Santa. Gifts were more likely to be wooden chess sets or solitaire sets from local markets. In the UK our friends would get hyped up about what they were getting months in advance but we didn't really care. Having loads of possessions would have been impractical. We carried things that we would use. On reflection, Paul and I can remember presents we got when we lived in Meadow Close.

I remember a BMX, a Game Boy and other stuff, but in the years we travelled we can't remember one present we got; they were unimportant. What mattered on Christmas Day was spending time with family – and we did.

We woke in the morning to glorious sunlight. We had a relaxed breakfast in the hotel and exchanged gifts before we headed down to the beach. The hotel had surfboards and kayaks for guests to borrow and we grabbed some boards. We had never been taught to surf but had tried it in India and knew the basics. As ever, Dad was game and joined in, paddling out with us and waiting in the swell for the right wave to pick him up and carry him back to shore. In true Forkan style, none of us gave up until we'd mastered the techniques and although we weren't as graceful as some of the other die-hard surfers who were in the water with us, we still managed to ride the waves and spent several happy hours clumsily splashing around.

Dad particularly enjoyed the challenge. He was approaching his mid-fifties at the time but had a young head on his shoulders and what he lacked in youth, he made up for with enthusiasm.

Mum watched him and smiled. They were best friends and had managed to raise six kids together while maintaining the free-spirited sense of adventure they'd had when they were young.

As the day wore on, Dad showed little sign of coming to shore.

'It'll take a tidal wave to bring him in,' Mum laughed at one point.

With Dad riding the surf, Paul and I played cricket and football on the beach until, eventually, it was time to go back, get changed and go for Christmas dinner. Dad paddled to shore with a grin on his face.

'We'll do a bit more of that tomorrow,' he said.

The hotel had laid on a special Christmas evening meal. There were decorations, a tree, tinsel and fairy lights. The waiters were all wearing Christmas party hats. The food was Italian-themed and delicious. The hotel had a Mediterranean feel to it with whitewashed walls and terracotta-tiled floors. With the smell of garlic and basil and the sound of carols playing softly in the background and the sea in the distance, we could have almost been on the Amalfi Coast. The owner flitted between guests, talking to an elderly Italian couple in his native language and switching to perfect English for everyone else.

He was a big football fan and had Italian flags and pendants displayed over the bar. He came over and talked to us about football for a while. The season in the UK and Europe was in full swing and we'd been following it closely.

People were in couples or groups, wishing each other happy Christmas and enjoying the warm evening. There was no TV on and everything seemed peaceful and relaxed.

Dad had his mobile phone with him and called Nan. Then he called Marie. She was at home with Liam and I could tell Mum and Dad missed not having her there. They were looking forward to the wedding. It would be the next big family affair we all attended and I wondered what we would all be doing then. I suspected our travels would be over.

We played chess and, later in the evening, the young Canadian wandered over with the Risk board for a game. Paul and I played him and he asked us about our travels and what we were planning on doing after Sri Lanka. Neither of us really knew. Paul would finish school and I would probably get a job with Dad helping with his website. I couldn't really imagine a life where I didn't travel though.

Jo was due to leave around midnight. She had a long journey ahead of her. She had a taxi booked to take her to Colombo from where she was due to fly two and half hours back to India and then catch a connecting eight-hour flight to the UK, arriving home late on Boxing Day.

When the taxi arrived to get her, we were all tired. It was quiet and chilled. There were no more than twenty people in the hotel in total and some of them had gone out while others had gone to bed. There were just a few left sitting outside, talking and drinking. We went to Jo's room to help with her bag, then walked out the front of the hotel. She hugged Mum and Dad. They wished her a safe flight and happy Christmas. She climbed in the car, which pulled away. We waved as the red lights of the vehicle disappeared down the main road into the Sri Lankan night. We turned and walked back to our villas. Mattie and Rosie were exhausted and Mum and Dad gently guided them indoors to get them into bed. They turned and smiled at Paul and me.

'Happy Christmas, boys,' they said in unison.

It had been a perfect day.

CHAPTER 8

26 December 2004

THE SUNLIGHT STARTED to filter into the room sometime after 6.30 a.m. By 8 a.m., I was beginning to wake up. I lay still, wrapped in a soft blanket with my eyes closed, listening to the world outside. It was quiet. Most of the guests were still in their rooms after the festivities of the previous night. I could hear a few early risers outside and could make out the sounds of breakfast being prepared. In the background I could hear the sea. Paul was fast asleep in the bed on the other side of the room, as was his habit in the mornings. He was fifteen, I was seventeen and, like a true teenager, he would have slept in until noon most days if he was allowed. He had never been a morning person. For some reason I had always liked getting up early and as we often shared a room, most mornings I would wake him up, usually just for a laugh.

I thought about what we would be doing that day. There were no plans for outings and Dad was eager to get back on the surfboard, so it would be a free, easy day on the beach, some swimming, some surfing and possibly a trip into town later.

Rubbing the sleep from my eyes, I turned over and swung my legs over the side of the bed. My feet hit something wet. I looked down, puzzled. A layer of water covered the tiles on the floor. It was only around a centimetre deep and was rippling gently across the room. We were so near the beach, I assumed that the tide had come in too far, or that a big wave had washed over the tide line into the complex. I didn't panic. I was bemused more than anything and jumped out of bed, splashing into the water to grab my bag and throw it onto the furniture to keep it dry. There was already water lapping around it. I didn't fancy having to hang everything out to dry and not having any clothes to wear.

I shouted across to Paul, who was oblivious to what was happening.

'Paul, the room is flooded; get your bag on your bed!'

He grunted and turned over.

'Come on,' I told him, 'your stuff will get soaked.'

'Leave me alone,' he groaned finally.

I stood in the warm water for a few seconds, looking around. It was murky, as if it had been churned up, and not at all like the crystal-clear sea that we had previously snorkelled in. As I surveyed the room, the water began to gently recede back out under the door, as if being sucked away. It was eerie, like somewhere a plug had been pulled out. Everything sounded different. The birdsong that accompanied every glorious sunrise was absent and there was no rhythmic ebb and flow of waves. Everything was still and quiet. It felt tense.

Intrigued, I followed the water out through the door and into the sunshine towards the beach for a couple of feet. It had crept up and into several of the bungalows a row back from the beach front. Mum and Dad's room would have flooded too. A few of the other guests were outside and equally puzzled. Behind me, further back towards the main hotel and restaurant, I heard a commotion. I turned and saw the elderly Italian couple who were staying in one of the two-storey buildings on their balcony screaming and pointing towards the sea. I looked in the direction they were gesticulating and, as I did, the German father who was staying in one of the other buildings with his wife and child ran past from the beach. He was clenching his toddler to his chest and straining to run as fast as he could. He made no sound, just his desperate breaths and the urgent padding of his bare feet on the sand. His face was set in an expression of horror, sheer panic and grim determination. Whatever it was he was running away from, he was moving as if his life depended on it. He looked like he'd just stared into the jaws of death. He didn't look at me as he passed. Nothing else mattered to him except getting away from what he'd just witnessed. His expression sparked some primal instinct in me. My mind flipped. I knew instantly that some great peril was about to befall us. Then, in the distance, I heard it. A rumble, like a train hurtling towards me. A breeze started to pick up from the seafront. The palm fronds in the trees began to move. I felt the ground vibrate. A jolt of adrenaline shot through me. I needed to act. Something was coming; something vast and powerful.

My first thought was Paul. I darted back into the room through the open door.

'MOVE, MOVE, MOVE,' I screamed. Paul's eyes flicked open wide in shock as a loud noise, which appeared to come from everywhere at once, filled the room, building quickly to a crescendo. And the world turned to chaos. There was no time to absorb what was happening. I turned to face the doorway when it hit.

The sea, in all its anger and brutal violence, rose up and wiped out the world we knew. Without warning, and in an instant, a wall of water slammed into the building, it forced its way into the room, crashing through the window. I reacted instantly and raised my arms to protect my face. Shattered shards of glass sliced through my bicep and forearm. I didn't feel it, I didn't have time to think about what was happening, but I knew I had to stand up and I braced myself against the torrent. The water was dark and impenetrable. I couldn't let myself get washed over into it as it cascaded into the room. Everything I'd learned about going with the current was wrong. The forces swirling around were so powerful, I knew they would snap me in half like a twig if I let them take me away. All that mattered in that instant was fighting it and staying upright.

The water rose within seconds. The room was a maelstrom. The furniture was picked up and smashed around me. The force tore the sink from the wall, pulverizing it into jagged pieces. I grabbed the wall for support and called to Paul, who had managed to get to his feet just in time and was behind me.

'Get out!' I shouted.

The water was waist-high and rising fast. The higher it got, the more chance it had of carrying us away. We needed to get out. If we stayed in the room we wouldn't get out alive.

I pushed forward, through the door. I couldn't comprehend what was happening around me. The world had been submerged. It was sinking. Our picturesque tropical resort was being dragged under a churning vortex that engulfed everything and was brown with silt and mud. Through the door I could see the water surging inland full of fury and roaring hatred. The noise was deafening. And in the middle of the horror Paul and I struggled to get clear of its grip.

There was no time to assess the wider situation. All that mattered were the few square feet in my immediate vicinity. I needed to get higher. I needed to keep my balance and escape the room. The door had been ripped off its hinges and through the doorway I could see that the water had risen up the veranda wall at the front of our accommodation and was pouring over the top. The structure offered a raised area to stand on and I lunged forward to grab the supporting metal pole at the end of it. With the other hand I grabbed Paul and pulled myself up so I was partially out of the water. I kicked forward and managed to get my feet on the wall, which by then was totally submerged, and as I did I pulled Paul clear of the room. Above me there was another metal bar which was connected to the roof and ran parallel to its edge. I reached across and gripped it. As I did, I felt the wall I stood on disintegrating beneath my feet like sand being blown by the wind. I was left suspended by one arm. With the other hand I was clinging on to Paul. The water tried its hardest to drag him from my grip. I don't even know how I did it, perhaps the water had given us an extra lift, but I found hidden reserves of strength and held onto him while I pulled us both up out of the water and on to the roof. We clambered barefoot over the lip of the gutter and scrambled in a panic as high as we could to try and get as far from the water as we could. We were both shaking in shock.

After the initial roiling sledgehammer wave, the water continued to come in surges and crested over the bottom edge of our flimsy refuge. The building was engulfed. The water picked up debris and ripped tiles away inches from our bare feet. The roar was punctuated by crunching and scraping as debris was carried by the irresistible current below the surface. Buildings melted away in its wake and uprooted trees became battering rams, smashing into obstacles that stood in their way. We crouched above it, helpless. It was terrifying. I thought about my life, my childhood and my travels. I thought about death.

Then, as quickly as it had started, the surge stopped. The noise abated and the water seemed to calm. It could only have been a few seconds, but time seemed to slow. Up until that point, my only focus had been survival and so for the first time, with the immediate threat in stasis, I took stock of the situation and looked at the wider surroundings. And it was like nothing I had ever seen before. The sea had replaced the land. I thought the world had ended. It was beyond comprehension. There was debris floating everywhere. The world was a soup of twisted shapes and brown water thick with mud. Trees were lodged in buildings; planks, sunbeds, wires and metal crushed together in a floating carpet of debris. Initially I couldn't see a soul. Some of the larger trees that fringed the beach were still standing and as I looked across at them something caught my eye. There was a figure in the higher branches a few feet above the water line. I looked closer and realized it was a small white boy. It was Mattie. He was around fifty yards away and he was calling out, petrified.

I snapped out of my awestruck horror and grabbed Paul's arm.

'It's Mattie, he's in the trees.'

I called over to him.

'Hang on, I'm coming to get you.'

Even from that distance I could see an ugly red smudge running down the front of his face. He was injured.

The only fleeting thought I had for my own safety was whether the power lines in the water would still be carrying electricity. I figured they would have short-circuited and slipped off the edge of the roof into the water, so told Paul to stay put and keep an eye out for any danger. I didn't want to be in the water any longer than I had to be, I had no idea what was under all the debris and I didn't want to think too hard about it. I powered towards Mattie, who continued to call out.

About halfway across, I started to feel a gentle current, this time it was heading back in the other direction, out to the direction of where the sea had once been. The debris I was picking my way through, which had been still moments earlier, began to move. The wave was ebbing, dragging everything it had picked up with it back to sea, me included. Under the surface objects started to bump against me. Some were solid, some were soft. I concentrated on my strokes. I swam faster, trying not to panic. I couldn't think about the repercussions if I didn't get to Mattie. My younger brother needed me.

The last few feet took all the effort I had and, when I grabbed a branch and pulled myself onto the trunk, I was exhausted. I didn't have the strength to haul myself up out of the water so I manoeuvred myself around to the side of the tree facing the current and let it pin me against the bark. I clung on as more debris banged past me.

Mattie was a few feet above me.

'Where's Mum and Dad?' he cried. He was in shock, shaking and crying. There was a deep gash in his forehead. The blood had run down his face and dried in streaks. I knew I needed to keep him calm.

'Don't worry, Mattie, they'll be somewhere safe,' I told him between gasps for breath. 'We'll be OK. Just hang on tightly.'

The water level subsided as the wave slithered back out to sea, sucking debris with it, leaving other twisted wreckage ashore. It revealed a scene of utter devastation. Everything had been destroyed. The landscape had changed completely. Buildings had been erased, those that remained were piled with debris and loose vegetation. Everything was covered in a layer of mud and wet sand.

I helped Mattie climb down from the tree. I was covered in cuts and grazes, but felt nothing. The gash on my arm was deep and dripping with blood. We were both stunned and terrified that the water would return. Paul climbed off the roof and picked his way through the wreckage to us. We had no idea what had happened and the three of us stood numbly, trying to take it in.

From beginning to end, the whole event was subsequently timed at around ten minutes, but in that short space of time our lives changed for ever.

I ventured a few yards further out past the buildings onto the beach to an area that afforded an uninterrupted view up and down the coastline and further inland. The scene that unfolded was the most shocking I had ever witnessed. It was catastrophic, like something from a disaster movie. For as far as I could see, there was destruction. I couldn't identify an area for miles in any direction which hadn't been annihilated. The whole coastline had been wiped out. Real fear struck me. I knew in that instant that we would have to fight for our lives to get out of the situation. I had no idea what had caused the wave, but it was very obvious that the force of the water had inflicted unimaginable damage. The road that ran behind the hotel had been washed away and from my vantage point I could see the damage had spread far inland. Everything had been utterly flattened.

I knew we were in trouble and I knew we needed to find Mum, Dad and Rosie.

'Where did Mum and Dad go?' I asked Mattie.

'I don't know. They got Rosie and me out of the room and lifted me into the tree,' he replied.

'They'll be waiting for us somewhere,' I told him.

I put emotions aside, buried the dread that was threatening to rise up in me and tried to be as logical as possible. First we needed to get Mattie to safety. The two-storey pagodas in the hotel grounds were still standing and I led him over to one of them, where the elderly couple were staying. They were on the balcony, weeping in shock.

'Please look after my brother,' I asked, 'I need to look for my parents.' I didn't know if they spoke English, but they understood what I was saying and nodded. Mattie climbed through the debris piled at the bottom of the stairs that ran up to their front door and went up and stood on the balcony with them. I told him to watch the sea and call to us if he saw the water starting to rise again. I wanted to give him a task, something to keep his mind and attention away from the scenes around him.

Then Paul and I went to our parents' room. I didn't know what we would find, but it was the obvious place to begin looking for them.

The door was hanging from one hinge and the glass in both the windows had gone. I peered inside. Like our room, it had been wrecked. The beds and furniture were upended and smashed. The floor and furnishings were sodden. I crouched down and started to look through the debris on the floor. I was looking for anything I could salvage that might help us. I knew by the scale of what I'd seen along the coast that whatever had happened was huge. For all I knew, the world had ended. I found Dad's mobile phone. I tried to switch it on but it was dead. It had been smashed and submerged in water. I opened the back and took out the SIM card. I also found a traveller's cheque signed by Mum. I folded it and put it in the pocket of my swimming shorts with the SIM card. There was nothing else left in the room and no sign of our parents or Rosie.

Outside, people had started to emerge, each in various states of shock. Many were like zombies, aimlessly wandering through the wreckage of a broken world. Others stood still, trying to comprehend what had happened. Most were lost in their own worlds; some were just mumbling to themselves, others were screaming and crying, trying to find loved ones they had lost. We asked the ones who looked capable of rational thought whether they had seen our parents. No one seemed capable of helping, so we set off on our own. I worked out very early on that we would get little help from the older people. We started meticulously searching the grounds, rooms and main buildings, one by one, looking for clues as to where the rest of our family was. No one stopped and asked if we were OK or whether we needed help.

We carefully rummaged through the debris and broken glass and searched in the buildings that had remained intact on the complex. All the while there was a palpable tension in the air, a fear that the waters would come back. Periodically we went to check on Mattie. When we were satisfied we had looked as extensively as we could, we decided to head inland. Our parents were not in the complex and I figured perhaps they had gone inland to higher, safer ground. I wanted to get Mattie somewhere safe too and thought it would be safer where there were more people. The ones we had come across up until that point were shell-shocked and senseless. It was around a mile to the centre of Weligama along the main coastal road, but from where we were that route was no longer an option. There was no road left. It had been swept away and all that remained were obstacles. As we walked out of the front of the hotel, it became even more apparent how powerful the water had been. Cars, vans and whole buildings had been picked up and dumped.

I looked around for an easier route. The steel rails of the railway that led along the coast had buckled and twisted, but the sleepers were still embedded in the ground and offered a convenient, negotiable pathway. I took Mattie's hand and we began trotting through the annihilated landscape.

It didn't take long until we encountered the first body. It was partially submerged in a pool of water and debris. A limb jutted out at a strange angle. Mattie pointed it out.

'What's that?'

I tried to divert his attention from it. I didn't want him to panic.

'It's OK, Mattie, just keep an eye on where you are running,' I told him. It was vital that he was kept calm. I didn't want the added complication of an asthma attack to deal with. However, the further along the coast we got, as we passed more densely populated areas, the more macabre the sights we began to see. The area immediately behind the beachfront hotels and restaurants was predominantly residential. It was where most of the workers lived; the waiters, cooks and cleaners who made a living servicing the tourist trade. And as we left the rail tracks and headed through these residential streets, we saw more and more bodies. There was only so much I could keep from Mattie. There were bodies by the side of the road and bodies washed up against the sides of buildings. Several empty train carriages lay on their sides by the side of the track, washed over like toys.

At one point we passed a statue carved into the rock by the rails. It depicted a man the locals claimed was the Leper King, an ancient ruler who cured himself of leprosy by drinking coconut milk for three months. There were meditating Buddhas carved in the tiara of the statue. Near the statue I could see a body under a mound of leaves and mud. I pointed out the Buddhas to Mattie while I guided him around the poor soul who lay in our path.

I couldn't protect him from everything and each of us silently registered the horror but we kept going. Along the way we saw other people wandering around. I've wondered since how we managed to stay cool-headed when the majority of the adults we encountered had gone to pieces. I think it was because of our travels and our upbringing. By the time we got to Sri Lanka we had been travelling for four years and we had spent a long time in India and witnessed some horrible sights in the cities. We'd seen extreme poverty and extreme human suffering. I'd seen child beggars, orphans and people with leprosy. Although what we witnessed in the wake of the wave was on a completely different scale, we had been exposed to suffering in the past. Most of the tourists we came across had not. They were just there on two-week holidays. We had grown accustomed to challenging situations and to the randomness that life can present when travelling. I imagine that gave us some rudimentary preparation for what we were experiencing and stopped us becoming overwhelmed. We also had a well-developed sense of independence. In conventional schools children are taught from a young age that whenever something goes wrong, they should find an adult. If you are bullied, go and find a teacher. If you are lost, go and find a policeman. We hadn't had a conventional upbringing and it was natural to accept that if we were to get out of the situation we were in, we had to take responsibility for ourselves.

Closer to the town centre, the chaos created by the water had been replaced by human chaos. It was as if an ants' nest had been stirred into action and there were hundreds of people in various states of panic, grief and shock, each in their own private world. The pervading sense of dread persisted; you could feel it in the air.

As we walked into the centre of town, there was no organization, no one was in charge, but people appeared to be congregating in the town's mosque, which was on high ground and tall. It looked like the safest place in Weligama and we followed the crowds; some were carrying bodies, many people had ugly wounds. We walked inside. It was bedlam; crammed with people. It stank of sweat and fear. The deafening sound of shouting and crying filled each room. The main hall was rammed full of people, and no one seemed to know what was going on. Injured people were slumped, bleeding, in corners and on the floor. Some were receiving basic first aid, but the place was overwhelmed. The wound in my arm needed stitches and Mattie's head wound needed attention, but I knew the place was unhygienic and we were not urgent cases. We looked in each room, trying to find white faces to see if any of them were our parents or Rosie. Paul and I continually reassured Mattie that everything would be OK. We asked people if they had seen anyone matching our parents' or Rosie's descriptions, but some just stared blankly back. We hunted through the temple for around half an hour but increasingly it became apparent that the search was futile.

We decided to head back to the hotel complex again. I was trying to second guess what our parents would do and wondered if perhaps they had arrived in town as we had, realized how chaotic it was and decided to go back to find us at the coast. Our journey meant retracing our steps through the town and along the railway line.

As we walked back to the sea, the death toll was starkly evident. The water left by the wave had started to dry up, revealing more of the horror. It was impossible to ignore. Back on the beach there was more activity. By then it had been several hours since the wave hit and, although there was still a fear that it would return, people were taking the risk to look for their lost loved ones and to start helping others. They had been shaken out of their shock.

By the time we walked back through the front gates, there were around twenty people milling around and we asked if anyone had seen our parents or our sister. No one had. We searched through the piles of debris again. We walked down to the beach.

I tried hard to remain positive; I couldn't entertain the thought that anything terrible had happened to Mum, Dad or Rosie.

On the beach there was a group of people in front of the surfers' hostel. A young couple ran over to us.

'Are you the brothers who were staying in the Neptune?' they asked urgently.

We nodded.

'Have you got a sister?'

My heart started racing.

'Yeah. Rosie,' I answered.

They turned and called excitedly to a group of people standing by the main doorway of the hostel.

'We've found them,' they yelled. The people by the door called inside the building to someone we couldn't see.

'Your brothers are here.'

I started running towards the door. I could barely hope to believe that Rosie was inside. So many people had lost their lives.

The door to the hostel was a pane of shattered glass. Inside, a narrow, debris-piled hallway led to a flight of stairs. I looked through the broken glass and saw my little sister walk down the stairs. She was wearing a swimming costume. When she saw me, she started to run and burst through the door crying. We threw our arms around each other and hung on, weeping. Relief swept through me. I didn't want to let Rosie go in case I lost her again. I've never felt so emotionally overwhelmed. To find someone alive in the midst of all the death was incredible. Rosie was only a child, she had always been the princess of the family, the youngest and the one we all looked after. I picked her up and she clung on to me tightly and buried her head in my neck.

'It's going to be OK,' I told her. 'We are going to get through this. Mum and Dad will be waiting for us.'

Paul and Mattie ran and joined us and when Rosie eventually let go of me, I checked her over for injuries. Like all of us, she was battered and bruised but she had sustained another injury which concerned me more. She had a very deep gash down the length of her arm. It had stopped bleeding and had been cleaned up by the people at the hostel, but it would need attention. She told us it didn't hurt. None of us had even mentioned our injuries. We were so full of adrenaline we didn't feel them.

I knelt down and gently asked Rosie if she knew where our parents were. She told me that they had got her out of the room when the wave hit, but that was the last time she had seen them. They had tried to keep hold of her, but the water had swept them away.

I asked the surfers where they had found her and they told me she had been standing under a tree, which she had climbed up to get away from the water. They also said how incredible she had been. She didn't panic, she hadn't crumbled or cried. She was a fighter, they explained; she was fearless.

I thought back to the adventures we'd had. We'd driven on roads on cliff edges and had trucks come at us with no barriers to protect us. We'd encountered deadly snakes. We'd surfed and trekked through jungles. We'd been in chaos in Delhi and Mumbai. We had a measured view of danger and it was helping each of us cope with the situation we were in. I said a silent thank you to Mum and Dad. Without the experiences they had led us through, I questioned whether we'd be alive.

We hadn't eaten or drunk anything all day. We found a bottle of Coke on the floor in the restaurant of the surf hostel and shared it while we discussed what to do next. We knew we were not going to find our parents there. Again I presumed that they had gone inland, which was where most people were then heading. There was nothing for anyone at the seafront and no shelter. We spoke to the rest of the survivors on the beach who were mainly European holidaymakers. We told them that people were congregating in the mosque in town and that if help were to come, it would probably reach there first. It was also on high ground.

'It's safer than staying on the beach like sitting ducks,' I said.

The consensus was that we were right and the group agreed it would make more sense to be among people. We were the only ones to have ventured from the beach into the town and knew the way.

'The road's gone,' someone said.

I explained that there was a route along what was left of the railway.

'We'll show you the way,' I offered. With that I put Rosie on my back and the four of us headed back into town. A band of around twenty survivors, all of them adults, followed.

CHAPTER 9

Gotta Get Through This

MUM'S WORDS RANG in my ears.

'No matter what else happens, Mother Nature is the one thing that can change in an instant and flip your world around. Nature is the most powerful thing there is.'

There had been no warning. No tell-tale tremors. There was nothing. The destruction was immediate and complete. I'd vaguely heard of tsunamis, or tidal waves, but it was uncertain what had happened and what had caused the water to rise so violently. It obliterated everything in its path. I wondered whether somewhere out at sea an atomic bomb had been detonated.

As we led the band of survivors along the rail tracks they were quiet, some were slack-jawed in shock, unable to comprehend what they were seeing. Many were injured; battered, cut and bruised. A middle-aged German lady had broken her leg. It was obvious to see: swollen, purple and twisted at the knee at an unnatural angle. She was supported by two others. She wept and howled with pain.

Progress to the town was slow and there were more people around as we entered the outskirts, stumbling around the ruins of what had been their homes, searching for possessions lost to the water, searching for people, crying over bodies. Paul and I kept talking to Mattie and Rosie all the way; we tried to keep their attention focused on positives rather than the misery around them. Some in the group were emotionally stronger than others. It was obvious that some were on the verge of mental collapse and would periodically break down, especially if they were left alone with their thoughts.

Paul and I couldn't afford to allow ourselves to be overcome. We were focused on finding our parents. At that point it hadn't crossed our minds to crumble. We couldn't anyway, because we had the younger ones to look after and we needed to lead from the front. Mattie's asthma compounded the problem, and we needed to keep him calm. His head wound was manageable, as was the cut on my arm. The blood made them look worse than they were. Rosie had a massive gash on her arm that was the worst injury of the lot. It was so deep you could see the muscle. But she didn't complain.

We reached Weligama for the second time at around 2 p.m. It was busier and even more frenzied than it had been before, full of desperate and confused people. Many were injured and in need of medical help. Some carried bodies. Everyone was on edge, terrified that another surge would sweep in. Many people were heading in the same direction, drawn to the focal point of the main town centre from the tourist areas at the seafront. As we walked up a road on the outskirts, people started to run past us screaming. Someone, somewhere had heard or seen something and panicked. The panic spread like a contagion and started a stampede. It came from behind and in seconds scores of people were sprinting past, running away from an unseen danger up to the town. Paul and I picked up Rosie and Mattie and started running too. Along the way we had managed to scavenge some items we felt would be useful such as clothes and tools, but we dropped them and ran with everyone else as fast and as far as we could until our legs burned with effort and our lungs hurt. Eventually the stampede slowed and then stopped as people realized it was a false alarm. Exhausted, I squatted down and tried to catch my breath.

All around there were upended cars, vehicles in the sides of houses, houses with just one wall remaining, boats wedged into trees. Everywhere distraught people were weeping. It was as if normality had been reversed. In the UK, a person in a public place in obvious distress elicits a response. Usually someone will stop to help. But in Weligama everyone was in pieces. The few people who were calm appeared strangely out of place.

By the time we arrived back at the mosque, the situation had worsened considerably because more people had brought bodies to leave there and more injured people had arrived to seek help. The ground floor was the worst because that was where the people who were too badly wounded to get upstairs were. Many had just collapsed on the floor. It was hard to tell if some of them were dead or alive. Injuries ranged from broken and shredded limbs with bones sticking through flesh, to trauma and crush wounds. Bodies were lined up inside and outside. The group dispersed and we went inside to look for our parents again and ask people if they had seen them. As there were so few Westerners in the area, it made the search mercifully easier as we could concentrate on looking for the white people only. We hurried past the horrific sights and checked through the ground floor quickly.

In a room upstairs there was a man with a needle stitching people's wounds. He was crouching on the floor, sweating and grimy. He had one needle. He saw us as we approached and glanced at my and Rosie's arms. He gestured to me, pointed at my arm and made a stitching motion. He walked towards us.

'No, no!' I ushered him away.

I had no idea whether he was a doctor. There did not appear to be anyone medically qualified in the whole place. There was no system, no triage. People were just helping out as best they could. Those who were able helped those in need. The man had no proper medical equipment; it appeared he only had the one needle, which I guessed had been used to sew up countless other wounds. I knew enough to know how risky that was. I certainly wasn't going to let him loose on me and my sister.

We continued to search room by room, asking anyone who looked European whether they had seen anyone fitting Mum's or Dad's description. No one had.

We went back downstairs to the main room, which looked like some sort of battlefield hospital. It was noisy and smelled of sweat and blood. The air was cloying, people were crying and shouting, distressed and in pain. There were hundreds of them crammed into the building. Some were on blankets or mats, others were just laid out on the floor.

I managed to shut out the noise and keep focused. It would have been easy to be overwhelmed by the surroundings. Maybe growing up in such a loud raucous family helped in some way.

When I was a kid I learned to shut out the noise of squabbling siblings; it was the only option if I wanted peace and quiet.

A few years before we found ourselves in Sri Lanka, there had been a popular song that got a lot of airplay on the radio; 'Gotta Get Through This', by Daniel Bedingfield. The words from the chorus started to loop through my mind: 'I've got to get through this, I've got to get through this,' I repeated to myself. It became the mantra I focused on as I led my siblings through the rows of injured and bereft in search of our parents.

I saw one of the older German couples from the group we had walked up from the beach with. They were sitting on the floor, against a wall in a room on the second floor. They were uninjured but were not helping anyone. They were sitting and waiting to be helped, clearly upset by what was going on around them. Then the lady did something that I will never forget. She reached into a pocket, pulled out a Toblerone chocolate bar and calmly sat there eating it. I was suddenly reminded how hungry I was. Apart from the Coke, we'd had nothing to eat all day. She made no effort to offer anything to any of the desperate people around her. It turned my stomach. It was one of the most selfish things I have ever seen anyone do.

'Why aren't you sharing it out?' I thought. I could feel anger rise up inside me. It was a display of the other side of humanity: ignorant thoughtlessness and disregard for the suffering of others. There were kids in there with her who would have been starving.

We had been in the mosque for quite some time and it was apparent that our parents were not there. I decided I needed to look further afield.

I found an empty bit of space in one of the upstairs rooms and sat the others down while I crouched down in front of them.

'Everything is going to be OK. You guys need to stay here while I go and look for Mum and Dad, OK?'

They nodded anxiously.

'Paul, look after them. I'll be back in a few hours.'

I hoped there would be some form of administrative centre in another part of town that hadn't been affected by the water, somewhere people could go to find their loved ones. I hurried out of the mosque, leaving the others. I had no doubt that somewhere out in the turmoil Mum and Dad were together and were looking for us too. It didn't occur to me that anything bad had happened to them. They were indestructible.

Outside in the street, I started to ask people for information.

'Where are people going for help?'

Most didn't understand me. It was upsetting and frustrating. The longer the day went on, the more anxious I was to find Mum and Dad.

People shrugged or ignored me, lost in their own problems.

I turned and saw a boy behind me. He was Sri Lankan, smaller and skinnier than me but he looked around the same age. He was on a bicycle. He lived in the town.

He spoke English.

'Are you OK?' he asked, glancing at my arm.

I looked down at the wound.

'Yeah,' I nodded. 'I'm trying to find my mum and dad.'

'I've lost my mum,' he said. 'I don't have a father.'

He looked me in the eye.

'I'll help you,' he said. 'We'll look together. We'll be brothers.'

He afforded me a small smile. I nodded.

'Do you have another bike?' I asked.

He gestured around him as if to say 'take your pick'. The streets were full of debris and as bikes were one of the main forms of transport in the town, there were washed-up ones everywhere. It was easy finding one. I picked one which looked like it was operational out of a pile of twisted metal and rubble and jumped on.

'Where are we going?' I asked my new friend.

'Police,' he said. I followed as he pedalled off.

As we rode together, he explained that he had spoken to some of the locals who had told him that there were meeting points set up at the police station and also at a hospital a few miles out of town.

The police station was on the outskirts of town and it only took a few minutes to get there. It was a small building; there were a few police officers in it trying to maintain some form of order or system. There were crowds of people milling around outside and it was obvious that the staff there were totally unprepared for the scale of what had happened. They didn't know what was happening. People were getting frustrated, shouting and asking questions no one seemed to have the answers to. Bodies had been taken there as well and were lined up at the side of the building.

I pushed my way through the crowds with the boy and we got to speak to one of the policemen inside. My friend spoke in the native language and asked about his mum and my parents. The officer shook his head. One of the walls at the front of the police station was covered in pieces of paper. I looked more closely and saw each one had writing scribbled on it.

'For missing people,' the boy explained. The notes were messages from people who had lost others to let them know they were alive. Some had fallen off and were blowing away in the breeze. No one was registering the information properly.

'We'll go to the hospital,' the boy said.

We pedalled out of town, past where the wave had hit and into the countryside. Occasionally a vehicle raced past, ferrying injured people to the hospital. We had to ride up a large hill to get to it. It was hot, I was hungry and for the first time that day I started to feel exhausted. It was around 5 p.m., nine hours after the wave had hit.

As we neared the hospital, I could see even from a distance that it was mayhem. It was roughly as big as a medium-sized UK hospital with several different wings. To the side I could see an area the size of several football pitches which appeared to be full of bundles of material piled in haphazard rows. As we got nearer, I realized they were bodies.

As we approached the entrance, the full horror of what was happening there unfolded. At the front the hospital had outgrown itself. The whole car park and entrance had been taken over by the dead and wounded. The site consisted of several buildings and in between these there were bodies and people being treated. The staff were completely overrun.

I dropped my bike and together the two of us picked out a way through the people. I focused on the entrance. My heart was hammering in my chest. I didn't want to look around me. I didn't know who was dead and who was alive. There was a police officer in the reception area and a couple of other security guards who were trying to keep some sort of order. Like at the police station, there were throngs of people asking questions and trying to find information. I got to the front and there was a table with pens and paper on it, people were queuing up to write their names and the names of missing people on them and there was someone there organizing things. It was the first time I'd seen anything resembling a system of registration so I wrote down Mum and Dad's names, who I was and where we had stayed.

I approached one of the guards with my friend and asked whether he'd seen a white man or woman. He looked overwhelmed and exhausted. He muttered something.

'He says "go and look",' the boy explained.

We went off together and searched the hospital, room by room. It was easier for me as I was only looking for white faces so I searched quicker and in the pandemonium the two of us became separated.

Everywhere there were people wounded and patched up with bandages. Some had beds, some were lying on the floor. The doctors and nurses were swamped and struggling to cope with the tide of misery around them.

I scanned each room, asking people whether they'd seen a white man or woman. Then, after about twenty minutes, someone directed me to another part of the hospital. They told me that they'd heard a white woman had been admitted and was being treated on one of the other wards.

My heart leaped. It was the first lead I'd had and I ran back through the hospital to where I had been directed, hopeful that I'd find Mum and Dad.

I ran into the ward and scanned across the faces lined up in the beds and on the floor, anxiously searching for a familiar one.

I saw the white lady. She had dark hair and bloody bandages around her leg. It wasn't Mum. I looked again in case I had missed someone. I walked through the wounded but there were no other Westerners there except the poor lady, injured and on her own. I turned and left the room.

Despondently I continued looking until I had done a complete circuit of the hospital. I became increasingly depressed and the realization dawned on me that to make sure I hadn't missed anything, I would have to search the only place left to look: the macabre makeshift morgue outside. I didn't want to see what was under the sheets but I had no choice.

Outside, others were going through the horrific task of searching for their loved ones among the dead. The bodies were laid in rows. Some were covered, some were not. I walked through them trying not to look too long at each one; just a glance to check for any that were people with white skin. There was nothing, no hope, just row after row of lives ended too quickly.

Then I saw him. I looked for too long and the image seared into my mind where it remained for a long time. He was a small boy. There was no cover on him. His body was frail and he was frozen in the position he would have been in when the wave hit him. He was curled up. His mouth was fixed in an eternal, silent scream. His eyes were wide with terror and his arms were up near his face to protect himself. It was horrible. I turned and ran.

The Sri Lankan boy was sitting where we had left the bikes. I could tell by the look of dejection on his face he'd had no luck and he knew by the ashen shock on mine that neither had I. Deflated, we rode back to Weligama in silence, where we wished each other luck and parted. Both of us had witnessed things we would never forget and yet we didn't even know each other's name.

It was twilight when I walked back into the mosque to tell Paul the bad news. I led him outside out of earshot of the others who had been waiting patiently for my return. I didn't want Rosie or Mattie to hear the details of what I'd seen although protecting them from the full horror of what was unfolding around us was futile.

Paul and I stood by the roadside talking quietly. I glanced over and saw a white man approach. He looked around forty-five and, like most people, wore a dirty T-shirt and shorts. He spoke to us in a Geordie accent.

'Hi, lads, my name is Tony. Are you the boys who were staying in the Neptune?' He seemed friendly and it was a relief to hear a UK accent.

We nodded.

'Can I have a few minutes of your time, please?'

He explained that one of the waiters from the hotel had some news and wanted to speak to us. He led us to a small single-storey building opposite the mosque. Inside it was hot and humid. There was no electricity and in the fading light I could see a group of locals sitting around, some on seats, some on the floor. They were talking quietly. I recognized some of the staff from the Neptune. There was a woman with them; it emerged that she was Tony's wife.

They were drinking tea and beckoned for us to sit down. One of the men offered Paul and me a cup each. We accepted them gratefully. As we sipped, we looked at the group expectantly. They talked among themselves. The waiter seemed upset and anxious. He looked at us sadly and then looked at Tony, pleading.

Tony took a breath.

'Lads, I'm so sorry, but it looks like they've found your dad. He was in the ice factory next to the hotel.'

He didn't have to spell it out; we knew they'd found a body. I didn't want to believe it was Dad.

'How do they know it is him?' I asked.

Tony went on to describe him; a tall white guy. I knew in my heart of hearts that it was true. The waiters all knew my dad, there was little chance they would have mistaken the man they'd found for someone else and there was no reason for them to lie to us. They were kind, decent people. They would not have told us if they were not sure.

'Do you want to go and see to make sure?' Tony asked gently.

I shook my head mutely.

Paul and I couldn't contain ourselves. We broke down, sobbing. Our heads dropped onto our knees and Tony and his wife grouped us together and hugged us.

'I'm so sorry, boys,' he said.

He didn't know what else to do or say. We sat like that for a while as the pent-up emotions of the day poured out of us. It was a luxury to let go for a while. But I knew we had to pull ourselves together for the sake of the young ones who were waiting for us over the road. There was no time for self-pity.

When we'd composed ourselves, we decided not to tell Mattie or Rosie. The less they knew, the better. We needed them to have hope and to keep going. Tony explained that there was another group of Westerners in the village and that, along with the Neptune's owner, they were going to try and get to the capital, Colombo. The owner knew people there who might be able to help. At that point no one knew how badly damaged the rest of the country was and how far inland the water had gone. (We later learned that in some places it had travelled miles.)

I didn't want to go. If Dad was dead, I didn't want to leave without Mum. Perhaps she was lost somewhere and needed us. I wanted us all to be together. But I knew I had to get us to safety and there was little hope staying in the ruins of Weligama. The situation was desperate. There was no food or water. Rosie and I both needed medical treatment and, from what I'd seen, the emergency services had collapsed. I knew if we were to survive we needed to get away. Paul and I agreed on a plan of action. We would tell Mattie and Rosie that Mum and Dad were going to meet us back at home in the UK and that we needed to get to the airport.

We left to get our siblings and, as we crossed the main road, a bus passed. It must have been taking survivors somewhere. Both of us looked at it and at the same time we screamed.

'Mum!'

We saw her sitting by one of the windows. We assumed she was going off somewhere looking for us.

Adrenaline and relief surged through me and we both ran off after the bus, screaming for it to stop. Even though we were emotionally drained, hungry, thirsty and exhausted, we managed to sprint to the vehicle and banged on the side of it, screaming until the driver noticed and stopped. He opened the doors at the front and we ran on.

'Our mum's on here,' we told him breathlessly as we ran down the aisle checking each passenger. Blank faces stared back. Mum was nowhere to be seen. We couldn't understand. We'd both seen the same thing. We were convinced she was there and looked again, becoming increasingly agitated.

'She's on here,' I said. 'I saw her.'

We couldn't understand it. We'd seen her as clear as day, yet no one on the bus looked remotely like her. We were crushed. It was devastating to realize she wasn't there and, after we'd climbed off the bus, we broke down and wept by the side of the road. 'Gotta get through this. Gotta get through this . . .' I repeated the mantra over and over in my mind. I lifted my head and looked at my brother.

'Come on, Paul. Let's go and get the others.'

To this day we are both convinced that we saw Mum on that bus. I don't know what happened or why she wasn't there when we got on it. It is inexplicable. Once more we picked ourselves up and put the dark thoughts and fears aside. What mattered most was getting our younger siblings home.

CHAPTER 10

The Long Road Back

REUNITED WITH MATTIE and Rosie, we went to find the group who were heading up the coast to the capital. The youngsters had been waiting patiently for us and we told them nothing of what we'd learned in the house. We must have looked a wretched sight. Each of us wore swimming costumes which were covered in dirt. Our faces were smeared with filth and tears. Our bare feet were filthy and covered in cuts. It hadn't occurred to me that I'd spent the day without shoes. Years of beach living had thankfully hardened the soles of my feet.

It was twilight and, without electricity, people had started to make fires for heat and light. In the windows of buildings and in open spaces eerie light flickered, bathing the surroundings in yellow and orange, casting shadows of twisted debris. The smell of smoke and decay filled the air. It felt post-apocalyptic.

We still knew nothing of the damage the wave had wrought further afield. We had no idea that the devastation had spread throughout South-East Asia. Periodically we heard helicopters in the distance. I'd seen a few military ones earlier in the day and the flights continued in the dark.

We convened with the rest of the group, who were waiting outside the house. Tony and his wife were with the owner of the Neptune and some of the guests who had been staying there, along with some people from the group we had led up from the beach. The German couple with their toddler were there. The lady with the broken leg was also there. She'd been patched up, but she needed proper medical attention and was clearly still in a great deal of pain.

There remained a palpable fear that the waters would return and, as it grew dark, the owner, who seemed to be the leader of the group, explained that he knew somewhere safe on high ground further inland where we could stay the night. The following day he would try and find a vehicle. There were some cars and buses moving through the town by then so we assumed there were roads open somewhere. The owner said that he knew people in the capital who could help if they were still there and if Colombo was still standing. It seemed the most logical place to head to. As far as he could tell, Weligama was cut off and there was no indication whether help was on the way. So the plan of action was agreed.

The adults had managed to gather some supplies. We had some blankets, a torch, some water and some food in the form of dry crackers. We set off from the town, heading inland on an intact road and continued walking for about an hour and a half. It was pitch black, hard-going and painful. A few cars passed us.

Our destination was a partially completed house on a building site. The second floor was an open platform exposed to the night sky and accessible by a ladder. It was high off the ground. There were construction vehicles parked around the site.

One by one, we climbed up. The lady with the broken leg struggled and the men helped. There was very little conversation. Everyone was still in shock and emotionally and physically drained. Someone lit a fire and boiled up some water to which sugar was added. I accepted a cup gratefully and ate a cracker. Someone also had a bottle of whisky which was passed around. I was offered some but declined.

Paul, Rosie and Mattie wrapped themselves in blankets and people started to fall silent as exhaustion overtook them. But I couldn't sleep. My mind continued to turn over. I climbed down and sat on the porch at the front of the building, assessing everything around me.

I wanted to work out an escape plan if the waters came back. I tried to work out how sturdy the structure was and whether it would withstand an onslaught. Where was the best vantage point to keep watch? There was a JCB nearby. Would it be better to get on that? Where could I run to if the water came? How long would I have to get the others to safety? I stayed awake all night, watching the road we'd walked up and the trees on either side, listening for the distant thunder. I didn't want to sleep because the last time I went to sleep, I woke up to the wave.

I sat, watched and listened through the night until the sky began to lighten and the others began to wake.

After more hot water, sugar and crackers, several of the men set off back into town to try and commandeer a vehicle. The rest of us set about looking around in the light to see what we could scavenge from the building site. We found some containers and piping and started to siphon fuel from the vehicles. If we couldn't use it, we could barter with it.

As we waited, a few more vehicles passed by. None of them looked like they belonged to rescue services. They were driven by private individuals lucky enough to have a means of transport.

After a few hours, the adults who had gone into town returned in a small van. I didn't ask how they got it; I assumed the hotel owner knew someone who lent it to him. There were no seats in the back and it was a squeeze, but we huddled in on the floor, packed what provisions we had and set off on the journey.

A nagging guilt tugged at me. I worried about leaving Mum. I worried that she needed me. But Mattie and Rosie needed to get to safety and I knew that was what Mum would have wanted. I reasoned with myself that if I could get the youngsters somewhere safe, Paul and I could return and continue looking.

The journey was hampered from the start. The vehicle was old and rickety and the main highway up the coast had been washed away. Normally it would have taken a few hours, but we had to find different routes north. We drove over dirt tracks. Each time we got near the coast, we would have to turn back when we hit the tideline of destruction the wave had left. The journey took us further inland.

The van was hot and noisy. Each bump caused the lady with the broken leg to moan in pain. After several hours we stopped at a village where we asked for directions. We were told we needed to head further inland as the entire coastal area was decimated. We tried to barter and beg for food. Repeatedly we hit dead ends and had to turn back, retracing our route to the nearest junction and trying a different road. It was trial and error and the going was slow. Occasionally we passed other vehicles.

There was chaos inland too. We stopped at one shop as it started to get dark and no one had any money. We tried to explain to the man that we couldn't pay and asked for his goodwill. There was nothing for us. Unsure of how long it would be until provisions and help arrived, people were guarding what they had.

The afternoon wore on and it became increasingly obvious that we were nowhere near our destination. We drove on through a haunted landscape full of haunted people. We stopped in a town to rest. We were all exhausted and I was becoming increasingly concerned. We were in a bad way. We had hardly eaten or drunk a thing. I hadn't slept. The cut on Rosie's arm was beginning to redden with the signs of infection. We found some leaves which we cleaned with water and gently applied around the wound, tying them in place with string.

We were weak and fragile. We constantly had to pump up Mattie and Rosie to try and keep them positive. At one point, late in the evening, Mattie started to complain that his asthma was bad. We had been in the small, enclosed van all day. It was dusty and hot.

I couldn't begin to think of the implications if Mattie suffered a full-blown attack and I left the others and walked into the main part of town to try and find a pharmacy or a doctor. I asked several people and managed to make myself understood. I was directed to a chemist who spoke some English. I mimed what he couldn't understand and he kindly handed over a bottle of pills. I had no idea what they were and hoped that he had understood me correctly. I couldn't afford not to try them and rushed back to Mattie. The evening had turned cold and everyone grouped together to share heat. I gave my youngest brother the tablets and, after a while, they seemed to work. His breathing became easier.

For a second night people began to drift into fitful sleep. I was shattered. My nerves were frayed, but each time I closed my eyes and drifted off I saw the water smash through the door of the room in the Neptune and bolted awake. I was glad when morning came.

Once again we headed off, edging north towards our destination. Eventually the roads became easier. While the wave had affected the whole of the eastern side of the island, the north was less damaged than the south and eventually the roads opened up. They were buzzing with activity. Increasingly helicopters swooped overhead and military vehicles rushed past. The forest gave way to buildings. After two days and 200 kilometres, we had arrived in Colombo.

We stopped periodically to speak to people and get an assessment of the situation. We were told that embassies had set up help desks in hotels in the city and that foreign nationals were being advised to make contact with consular staff. Worryingly, we learned that all hospitals and clinics in the city were totally overrun.

I'd seen first-hand what that meant and I didn't want to take Rosie into an environment like the one I searched through in Weligama. The Neptune's owner had a solution. He knew a doctor in the city who could help and he drove us to his house. A few others in the group needed fixing up too.

The start of the family story.

Mattie at the front and,
from left to right: Rosie, Marie,
Paul, Mum, Jo, Rob, Dad.

Always exploring new cultures . . .
. . . and permanently on the move.

Being packed off for our
first school day in India.

Another tuk tuk adventure.

On the left of this picture is Ian, the young Irishman who Dad adopted in Goa and who recently got back in touch with us.

We were always out on the water.

Devastated villages and buildings along the coast from Galle to Matara, close to Weligama.
(Top © Raveendran / AFP / Getty Images. Bottom © Jimin Lai / AFP / Getty Images)

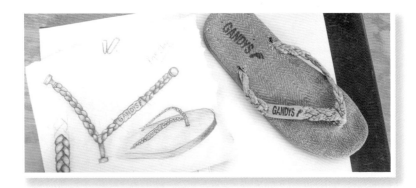

Original sketch of our first pair of Gandys made from jute with the unique rope strap.

One of the designs we produced in collaboration with Accessorize...
...and part of the range we worked on with the prestigious Liberty of London.

Orphans For Orphans is what makes us get out of bed.

Paul and Rob with Dilshan, a fellow tsunami orphan.

The team at Gandys.

Rob and Paul meeting HRH Prince Harry at Buckingham Palace.

(courtesy of Rhian Ap Gruffydd)

The doctor lived on his own in a quiet part of town. The Italian knocked on his door and thankfully he answered and was more than willing to help. He spoke English and ushered us inside where he had a proper look at Rosie's and my wounds.

'These need cleaning,' he tutted. 'They are going to get infected.' There was dirt and grit in our deep cuts.

The doctor took me to one side and spoke quietly but urgently.

'I have no anaesthetic,' he said. 'You need to go first and show your little sister that this will not hurt, do you understand? You need to show her how it is done.'

I understood. It would hurt, but I had to show no pain, otherwise Rosie would not go through with it. I also understood the Forkan sibling competitiveness. Rosie would see my bravery as a challenge and try her best to match it.

I sat in the doctor's chair and presented my arm. Carefully but purposefully, he started to dab away inside the deep gash with an alcohol-soaked swab. The stinging pain made my eyes water. I flinched and gritted my teeth. Then he started scraping out the cut and picking out the grit. It hurt beyond belief but I knew I couldn't let on to my sister. Then he started on my feet. I felt prickly and hot as I tried to keep calm.

Afterwards, the doctor patted me on the back.

When it was Rosie's turn, the German mother encouraged her and held her hand. The room went quiet when the doctor started.

Bless her heart, Rosie yelled the house down. She was in so much pain she was writhing, but she bravely let the man rinse out and scrub the deep wound. Mattie and Paul couldn't take it and started crying too. They were telling the doctor to leave her, but they knew it had to be done. It was traumatic to watch and everyone in the room was visibly upset.

After it was over we hugged Rosie and told her how brave she'd been.

The doctor had a mobile phone and, after he patched us up, I asked him if I could try it using the SIM card that I'd taken from Dad's phone as it had all Dad's contact numbers stored on it.

The doctor gave me the handset and I took the back off it and slid in the small plastic card I'd kept safe in my pocket.

I said a quiet prayer as I turned the handset on. It lit up and when I entered the contacts book, Dad's numbers were displayed. My heart raced and I scrolled straight down to Marie's number, pressed 'call' and breathed heavily as I heard the phone connect and start ringing at the other end. I had no idea what time it was in the UK.

Marie answered.

'It's me,' I said.

'Hello? Who is it?' She didn't recognize my voice.

'Me. Rob.'

'Rob?' she sounded shocked and confused. 'Rob, where are you? Where are the others? Are you OK? What's happened?' The questions tumbled out.

'I'm with Paul, Mattie and Rosie. We're safe. We're in Colombo with some other people.'

'Where are Mum and Dad?'

'I don't know where Mum is. We lost her at the hotel. Marie, you need to listen.' I began to tell her about Dad, but she didn't believe me so I stopped telling her.

'No way, Rob,' she said. 'They'll be together. Whoever said they saw him got it wrong.'

She said she'd been watching the news and told me that I needed to get the others and get home. I said we were going to the embassy to get help and she urged me to keep the others safe.

'I will,' I promised.

It was a huge relief to be able to speak to home and I took the SIM card out of the phone and placed it back in my pocket. The call lifted all our spirits. We just wanted to get back to the UK.

From the doctor's house we were driven into the city to the hotel that was acting as a muster point for foreign nationals. It was one of the big international ones and we were dropped off along with Tony and his wife. We said our goodbyes to the group and headed to the British consulate desk, which had been set up in the foyer. There were quite a few other Brits there and, as we waited to be seen, Tony wandered off and came back ten minutes later with a McDonald's. Safe at last, he'd used the last few emergency dollars he had. He didn't have enough to buy us all a meal but handed us a couple of burgers and Cokes.

'You deserve it,' he said.

We devoured what little there was as an official noticed us and came over to talk to us. We related the whole story to the official, that we'd lost our parents further down the coast and made our way up to Colombo. We explained that we had lost everything; all we had were the clothes on our backs, the SIM card and the traveller's cheque. We were ushered over to a quiet part of the foyer and invited to sit down. It didn't occur to us that our situation was unusual; we were four unaccompanied children. We'd seen so much chaos that we didn't know what normal was any more. But the staff were concerned and immediately started to make arrangements to look after us.

We didn't see Tony and his wife again. Like so many characters in those two days, they flitted through our lives and left a mark but disappeared. We were spirited away in a diplomatic car and taken to the ambassador's residence where we were met by a young couple in their early thirties who worked in the embassy. They were assigned to look after us and explained what would happen.

So much happened and at that stage I was so exhausted I was close to collapse. To this day I can't recall the names of those two people, but I remember their kindness.

The man told us that we would be taken back to the UK. The British government was in the process of chartering a plane which would take UK nationals home. But we had to stay in Colombo for a day so they could make arrangements for us when we got back. We were under the protection of the UK government and, until they found our parents, they had a duty of care to make sure we were properly looked after when we got back on UK soil.

The man also explained that, the following day, he was going to Weligama to look for our parents.

'I don't want you to worry, we'll resolve this,' he said.

The large, comfortable house was set in well-groomed gardens and was an oasis of calm. We were allowed the run of the place and had a hot meal. The lady went out and came back with a selection of new clothes for us. They didn't all fit but it felt good to be clean and fed. There was a TV in the large lounge but the couple made a point of putting on a selection of cartoons for us, I assume because every channel was full of disaster news. We were given access to the phone and called Marie again to tell her what was happening. She was liaising with the consular staff and the Foreign Office back in the UK to prepare for our arrival. We had no home to go to so she was going to look after us while the search for our parents continued. Until there was official confirmation that Dad had been found, there was still hope that we would all be reunited. I also called my Aunt Jenny, Dad's sister-in-law. I don't remember speaking to my uncle; I think he may have been too distraught.

That night I still couldn't sleep. Despite the comfortable surroundings, I felt anxious and found myself repeatedly evaluating where the exits were and where the nearest high point was.

The following morning I watched as the man kitted up with safety equipment and supplies. He was taking a 4x4 back down the coast to look for our parents. Paul and I wanted to go with him. We knew Rosie and Mattie would be safe, but at that point we were too weak to go back. We were tired, battered and bruised. After he left, we spent more time waiting in the house. We didn't venture out and weren't encouraged to.

Finally, the time came to head back to the UK but, before we left, the lady sat us down to talk to us.

'What has happened here is a huge event,' she said. 'There are reporters and journalists everywhere covering it. They will probably be interested in talking to you. Don't speak to them, no matter what they say or offer you.'

I was surprised. It hadn't occurred to any of us that we were a story or that anyone would be interested in us. We just wanted our parents back and we wanted to get home.

The lady's words were soon proved prophetic. When we walked through Departures at the airport, an American journalist ran over to us. He quickly introduced himself and said he was from the *LA Times*.

'Are the four of you alone?' he asked, but was ushered quickly away.

We were taken through passport control by the diplomatic staff and boarded the plane quickly. We had no belongings to check in. We wore ill-fitting clothes and looked drawn, battered and exhausted. We looked like the slum children we'd seen in India, wretched and frail. Rosie was ten, Mattie was twelve, Paul was fifteen and I was seventeen. Between us, we'd already witnessed a lifetime of horror. We were placed in the central four seats at the front of the BA 747 and given blankets. There were a few people with injuries, with limbs bandaged and cuts and bruises. Many of them must have been tourists who escaped the devastation as they carried hand luggage and wore clean clothes that fitted. We sat quietly as the plane took off. We weren't near the windows so I didn't see the view down the coast and the ugly scar that the wave had created across the land.

I don't remember much about the flight, but when we landed I felt relief. The seat-belt sign flicked off and everyone jumped up to get their hand luggage and get off the plane. The pilot's voice came over the Tannoy and told them all to sit down. They looked around, confused. The doors at the front of the plane opened and an officious-looking lady in a dark suit entered the cabin with two armed policemen behind her. She spoke to one of the stewardesses who then turned round and pointed at us. She walked over to us.

'I'm from the Foreign Office. Would you like to come with me, please?' she said politely. We stood and followed her as everyone on the plane looked on in amazement, wondering who we were. She took us straight off the plane and through the part of the airport where VIPs were taken.

'This is where David Beckham comes,' said one of the policemen.

The lady explained that there were family waiting for us and we were taken into one of the club lounges that had been emptied for us. We walked through the frosted-glass doors to be met by Marie, Liam, Jo and our cousin Lyn. It was a hugely emotional reunion, but I remember very little about it. They ran over to us and hugged us tightly. We all cried together.

'I'm so glad you're safe,' Marie sighed when she finally let go of us.

I don't know how long we were there and I can't recall what other conversations we had. There are parts that have been shut out of my memory and others that are crystal clear. It was a blur.

After a while, we were taken to waiting cars and driven out of a side entrance.

News travels fast. We didn't know it at the time, but our situation was already known by newspapers. There were reporters in Sri Lanka who must have spoken to survivors who in turn told them about the four British kids who had lost their parents. In an effort to protect us and allow us to come to terms with what had happened, the head of Scotland Yard had requested a media blackout and asked newspapers to respect our privacy and leave us alone. But while we were not approached, extended family and friends had already been contacted by reporters. This was the reason we arrived in such secrecy and were taken through the airport without seeing a soul.

From Gatwick we were taken to Frimley Park Hospital for check-ups and to have our wounds properly treated.

All the time I could feel exhaustion tugging at me and I became lethargic. My head was drooping. When the nurse who was stitching the cut on my arm asked inappropriately, 'Where have you guys been? You look like you've had a rough night,' it barely registered. How could you begin to explain what we'd experienced over the previous week?

From the hospital we were taken to Marie's two-bedroom house. The family liaison officer had arranged bunk beds to be delivered in anticipation of our arrival. There was a policeman in uniform stationed on the door. Everything was surreal. I couldn't take it in. We were back in the UK, we were safe but we needed police protection. The nagging guilt that I'd left Mum would not leave me.

We ate a meal. No one wanted to discuss what we knew about Dad. No one wanted to confront the truth, so we buoyed each other up and said they'd be found together and that our situation was only temporary.

With my siblings safe, I psychologically absolved responsibility to my eldest sister and allowed myself the luxury of switching off. My body felt like concrete, heavy and dense. I now felt every bruise and cut. My mind was giving up, everything was shutting down. I went to one of the bedrooms where I crawled into bed and passed out. I stayed there for a week and just slept, waking now and then to eat. I had done my job.

CHAPTER 11

Aftermath

IT **SEEMED SURREAL** being in the UK for all of us. In the weeks and subsequent months after we returned, we were in limbo. We didn't know how long we were going to stay with Marie or what the future held. Until there was official news, we kept hold of the hope that Mum and Dad would be found alive and would return. No one talked about the sighting of Dad. No one wanted to believe it, so we carried on as if they were still alive, lost somewhere in the maelstrom of human misery we had escaped from and which was unfolding each night on the news. In the cold British winter it seemed a world away.

Straight after we got back, Jo went back out to Sri Lanka to look for Mum and Dad. She booked a flight with her friend James and headed down to Weligama where she looked for clues as to what had happened. She was there for about a week but, in the chaos that was still unfolding, she found nothing.

Those first weeks passed in a blur and it's still hard to remember details about them. I remember the tiredness and the paranoia. I remember constantly trying to make sense of what had happened. I was annoyed about not coming back with our parents.

Initially it took time to recover from the exhaustion and battering we'd received. Rosie, Mattie and I sported scars where the wave left its mark. The injuries healed, but the emotional toll persisted. We were confined indoors for a long time, advised not to go out because of the continued media interest in our story. So we stayed inside, trying to avoid the news as none of it from South-East Asia was good. The death toll was immense and TV bulletins were full of footage of suffering.

At that point we didn't know what was going to happen to us. We assumed our parents would come home and they'd find somewhere to live. We were all quiet and weak.

We were introduced to a family liaison officer who came to the house every day. He was our link to the outside world. He was there to talk to the officials in Sri Lanka and in the Foreign Office and to coordinate things. He sat patiently with us and talked through the events in Sri Lanka to build up a story of where we had been and how we got back. He was passing the information on to the search parties and aid organizations in Sri Lanka in the hope it would help them locate Mum and Dad. We didn't talk to him about our fears that they had perished, it was too painful. Even though the tsunami was a massive global event, it wasn't mentioned in the house. Relatives came to visit. People got uncomfortable, no one really knew what to say. Any comment, no matter how well meant, always sounded glib. It wasn't a normal situation. We'd been caught in a natural disaster of unimaginable scale and lost our parents. There was nothing that could be said to make the situation any better so people didn't bother. Besides, our aunts and uncles were equally as distraught as we were. They had lost their brother and sister.

All of us were affected. Jo would have flown over the wave on her way back to the UK. If she'd looked out of the window at the right time she might have seen a change in the ocean below her as it raced across the world on its destructive path. She was devastated, as was Marie who had to show a positive face to the younger ones. She was getting married, but put her life on hold, including her job, until a resolution was found. She immediately said we would live with her until such time as our parents were found. There was no hesitation or doubt.

The policeman stationed on the front door stayed. It made us even more paranoid about what was going on. We were told that when we did go out, if we spoke to people, we shouldn't use our own names. So we had assumed surnames in the hope that we wouldn't be recognized. We stayed indoors for weeks. Someone went and found us a game of Risk to play. It was mid-winter outside and we sat indoors watching TV. We hated it. We loved being outdoors. We had all that freedom on our travels and suddenly it was gone.

We'd arrived back with nothing and needed clothes, food, bedroom furniture and all the other stuff children require. Arrangements needed to be made for Rosie, Mattie and Paul to go to school; they needed uniforms, pens, pencils, school books. Lots of stuff was bought. I wondered where the money was coming from. Marie had a decent job as a pharmaceuticals buyer, but to suddenly have to equip a large family was a big ask on an average wage. She also had to buy new furniture.

Living conditions were cramped. While Marie's house, in Farnborough, Hampshire, was a comfortable size for her and Liam, it was much too small for six. She didn't have a garden either. At twenty-two, she suddenly had two young children and two older teenagers to care for.

Help came from many different quarters and we are all grateful, to this day, to everyone who was touched by our situation. Family were brilliant, even though they were in shock and fearing the worst. Together we had made many friends in the New Forest due to the time we'd spent there and they rallied round. We'd gone to school and college in the area and, even though we hadn't lived there permanently, we had played cricket locally and it was perhaps the place in the UK where we had the strongest links, having been away from Purley for so many years. People helped out, dropping off food and supplies and did fundraising. The New Milton Leisure Centre where I'd worked and the New Milton Cricket Club where Paul and I had played, both held fundraising events.

The high school Paul had attended and junior school Rosie and Mattie attended raised money and had cake sales and raffles. Our mates did stuff too. I had a friend in a band who did charity gigs.

Other help came from unusual quarters. The owner of a big PR agency sent Marie money, telling her he wasn't interested in buying up her story, which was just as well because it wasn't for sale. He said he'd heard about our plight and wanted to help out. Several months later, however, his intention became clearer when he pressured Marie to sell out and she told him where to go.

We began to hear that many people we knew – all our family and friends – were getting approached by journalists who wanted information and to try to get messages to us. Usually they offered us the opportunity 'to tell our side of the story'. We were under no illusions that the prime purpose was to sell newspapers. They used any connection to us they could uncover: old school friends, Dad's former work colleagues and former neighbours. Not one person spoke. No one broke ranks. It happened daily and we were told to brief our mates. Everyone spread the word to be quiet. It was an incredibly emotional and difficult time, and we wanted to be left alone in private.

When I was at college before going to Sri Lanka I'd met a couple of close friends who are still good mates now, Kieron and Scott. They lived in the New Forest and were there for me, along with their parents, when I got back. Paul's best mate, Skinny, was down there too and Paul would go and stay with him while I went and stayed with Kieron and Scott. It was a place to get away to. After we came back from Sri Lanka, those guys didn't ask too many questions; they knew not to and it felt normal being with them.

Over the years, a lot of other mates played a significant role in helping us rebuild our lives. I often found friends easier company to be with than my own family because they were not directly affected by the events. Family were incredibly supportive and vital, but when we were all together in the confines of the house it was hard to get away from the overwhelming emotion of our situation. Sometimes we just wanted to be kids again.

It took a few months until we felt confident enough to start going out on our own after returning. Initially we were taken out by the family liaison officer who realized how unhealthy it was for us to be kept locked inside. He took us out to the local leisure centre. But because we had to be isolated from the public, he managed to convince the centre manager to close to the public for a couple of hours to allow the four of us to use the facilities. It was like being some kind of celebrity. We had the whole place to ourselves. We were taken there once a week and were able to do what we wanted. We swam and played badminton and basketball. Our identities were closely protected and we even had to register at the centre under different names. We used Liam's surname. It was like being in the witness protection scheme. Even when the police officer on the door finally went, we had other undercover officers stationed nearby watching us.

Paul and I went out on our own together for the first time a couple of months after we returned. We went to WestQuay shopping mall in Southampton. It also happened to be the first time we'd been out in a crowded place and it was by the sea.

I hadn't been there long before I realized it wasn't a good idea. I felt hemmed in by the crowds of people. It was too loud and too busy. I could feel the sea nearby but I couldn't see it and that made me nervous. I could feel the world closing in. My heart raced. I began to sweat. I started to see and feel things that weren't there. I heard the roar of the sea in my head. The noise of the shoppers became the noise of water. I was back in Sri Lanka fighting for my life. I was panting for breath. It took a huge mental effort to get to the door and to get outside in the cool air.

Paul found it very difficult to be in enclosed spaces too. I habitually looked for high ground and exit routes wherever I went. I still do, to some extent, but back then it became a preoccupation. I would panic if I found myself in a place where there was no easy way of making a fast escape. I felt happiest and safest on high, open ground.

A short while later I went out with friends who suggested we go to the cinema. I was apprehensive about going into a dark, enclosed space. I wanted to sit near the exits. My mates didn't realize how badly I had been affected and didn't really think about the choice of film.

'What are we going to see?' I asked.

'It's called *White Noise*, it's a thriller. It got good reviews,' they said.

I'd never heard of it. As the lights dimmed in the cinema, I could feel my pulse race and I tried to breathe slowly to stop the anxiety. When the movie started it became apparent that *White Noise* was a horror movie about dead people communicating with the living. It was the first film I'd been to see since the tsunami and it didn't take long for my friends to realize what a bad choice it was. They sat there, watching me carefully, hoping I wouldn't break down or flip out.

The emotional toll of what I'd experienced started to manifest itself in my dreams. I struggled to sleep. Most nights, as I started to drift off, my mind would take me back to the chaos and horror of Sri Lanka. One scene in particular played itself out repeatedly in my mind. I would find myself walking through the hospital car park just outside Weligama, picking my way through the shrouded bodies. I could hear people crying and feel the panic and overbearing sense of danger. And then I would stumble on him: the boy with his frozen scream looking up at me from the ground, a look of terror on his pale, lifeless face.

I continued to have flashbacks when I was awake. On another

occasion I was with friends in Bournemouth. We were in a restaurant by the sea when my mind started to slip back to Sri Lanka. It started when I walked in and began making escape plans. I looked for the exits and for the stairs to higher ground. I assessed how quickly I could run to another, taller building nearby and climb the stairs to the roof. I constantly thought about escape. I looked out at the sea and realized how powerful it was. I looked for waves on the horizon and then I was back in Sri Lanka, terrified and fighting to survive.

Eventually we had a counsellor. She was a South African lady called Joanne and was world-renowned in child trauma and natural disasters. Individually, we saw her often. We didn't talk about our fears or triggers to each other. Joanne tried to get us to block out and come to terms with some of the bad things we'd seen. She tried to get us to put them in context and understand them. In several sessions she hypnotized me and once I came out of a session and didn't know who I was. The counsellor had to call my sisters to come and get me because I was so disorientated. They were intense sessions and I was so young, I didn't really understand them. I learned later that she probably used a technique called eye movement desensitization and reprocessing (EMDR), which helps people suffering from post-traumatic stress disorder. The treatment involves controlling eye movements while recounting traumatic events. Apparently people suffering from PTSD have problems ordering and storing memories of the traumatic events that they have experienced. The brain jumbles these memories up and often they spill out into everyday life in the form of flashbacks. EMDR is supposed to help people store difficult memories in the right place in their minds so they don't intrude on reality.

The weeks turned into months and it was hard to make any plans. We were hearing very little news about the search from Sri Lanka. The task of finding and identifying people across the area affected by the tsunami was huge. We tried our best to stay positive. We continued to tell Mattie and Rosie that Mum and Dad would be coming home, they were just a bit lost.

It was frustrating. We were all in limbo. We didn't know what the future held and we were all stuck under the same roof. Increasingly, I went to stay with friends and also started to spend weekends in the caravan in the New Forest. We had to think about plans for the future, schooling for Paul, Mattie and Rosie and work for me, but it was hard when we didn't know what we were doing or where we would be going when Mum and Dad came back. I put all thoughts about what the waiters had told us about Dad to the back of my mind. No one seemed to be able to confront that eventuality.

I only really lost my temper once in those months. I was in a bank trying to get money out. I had no ID; it had all been lost. I had no card or passport. I tried to explain to the cashier that I had lost everything. I had some ID, I can't remember exactly what, possibly a birth certificate or letter addressed to me, but it wasn't the correct form required. There was a queue of impatient people behind me.

'Sorry, but we need to see your chequebook or passport before you can make a withdrawal,' the cashier insisted.

I was extremely wary of explaining why I had no ID on me and tried to appeal to her.

'Please,' I begged. 'I have some ID, you can see I am who I say I am. I have no other way of getting money. I have lost everything.'

She insisted.

'We can't release funds without the proper ID.'

I lost my patience and flipped.

'Look,' I breathed, 'I was caught up in the tsunami in Sri Lanka. You may have heard about it on the news! I've just got back, I've lost everything. I've lost my parents.'

The lady was gobsmacked and tried to calm me down.

'I'm so sorry, sir,' she said. 'I had no idea.'

She called her manager over and I was taken into a quiet room where the necessary arrangements were made.

I felt very uncomfortable telling people about my circumstances. I'd been advised to be secretive when we arrived back in the UK and over the years that stuck. It was not something I shared with strangers and, as time went on, many people I have met since had no idea about my past. I didn't want to be a victim and I didn't want to be treated any differently because of the circumstances I found myself in.

When it became difficult at Marie's house, I isolated myself and got away from it. We all dealt with it in our own ways. The young ones struggled the most. They would get very upset and rallying them round was hard work. Marie did it very well. We all showed our anguish in different ways. Paul and I had more of a drive to go and do stuff; we played cricket and football. We tried to fill our days with activities because when we were not doing things it hit the hardest.

As the weeks dragged on, I started to get an increasing sense that someone, somewhere was helping out. Marie was not working and yet our needs were being met. Our rooms were kitted out, we had clothes, we had food and money to go out. I knew enough about finances to realize that Marie would have struggled massively to provide for us all. She mentioned in passing that there were people helping. She let us know that people were being good to us and that we should be grateful, which we were. She acknowledged that our friends in the New Forest were being good and that people who knew us back in Croydon where we grew up were also helping out, but I had a nagging feeling something more was going on.

She'd drop hints.

'People really are wonderful; we are very lucky, you know,' she'd say.

I knew the clothes and furniture had to come from somewhere. Later she also had an extension built on the house and I knew the money for that came from somewhere too, but I didn't find out from where until many years later.

CHAPTER 12

Our Worst Fears Realized

WE HAD NO direct contact with anyone in Sri Lanka. Whatever communications were going on between the UK and the Sri Lankan government were dealt with by our family liaison officer. We all tried to get on with life as best we could while we waited for news. The longer it went on, the harder it got. No one wanted to face the fact that our parents might not be coming home. No news was good news.

At one point, about a month after we got back, there was a glimmer of hope. Tentatively we were told that there had been reports that someone on the island may have found someone who matched Mum's description. There were no more details; we didn't know if whoever they were talking about had been found alive or dead. We waited anxiously for more news but none ever came. The lead amounted to nothing.

It was hard to concentrate on anything, all of us were lost in our own worlds, waiting for news and waiting for our parents to return. The increasing death toll had become a global preoccupation. The numbers were simply staggering and hugely disheartening.

Then, three months after we returned, Marie called us all together one afternoon. The full details of what happened have been lost from my mind. Like many of the events from that time, I can only recall sketchy details. It is like a blur. There are mental blocks. It is something I have never wanted to remember.

Our eldest sister explained that Mum and Dad had been found. They were dead. It had been confirmed that the body found in the ice factory next door to the Neptune was Dad and Mum had been found nearby. I still don't know why it took so long to be confirmed. I can only imagine that the administrative infrastructure of the island had completely crumbled under the magnitude of the task of identifying so many bodies. From my experiences searching for our parents, I knew that the administrative services had been totally overwhelmed.

I remember everyone crying. We were all in pieces, trying to hug each other. The crying went on for ever. The young ones were inconsolable. Even though we each carried an unvoiced fear that bad news was on the way, it still didn't make the hammer blow of reality any less forceful. It felt like my heart had been ripped out.

My grief was mixed with a lot of guilt. I believed I should have stayed out there looking for them. I shouldn't have gone to Colombo. I should have carried on searching. I was haunted by the belief that Mum may have been trapped and injured somewhere and needed my help. I felt I had let her down and abandoned her.

Those feelings had surfaced in the months leading up to the confirmation of our parents' deaths and in counselling I was told that there was nothing I could have done and that I took the right course of action. Joanne tried to get me to accept that I did all I could, but that doubt remained and it still does to this day. I still question whether I could have done more.

There were no details about what happened to Mum. All we know is that Mum and Dad battled to get Mattie and Rosie out of the room and then they went. Dad was washed into the factory but I don't know whether Mum was injured somewhere and needed help or whether she managed to walk to find us. Sometimes I want to know, other times I feel it is best to leave the details alone.

I try hard not to revisit the weeks after we discovered that we'd been orphaned. We all mourned. The pain of loss was indescribable. We all felt completely empty, but we tried to look after each other. If one of us was particularly down, the others would rally round. We all tried to protect the youngsters as best we could. Like everyone, they grieved in stages. One minute they would be fine, playing or watching TV, the next something would spark a memory and they would be distraught. It was so hard to come to terms with the fact that we would never see Mum or Dad again. They had been such a huge part of our lives; they had shaped and moulded us all.

The one comfort we did have was the knowledge that they had died together. They were a unit, a solid team, and had been together for so long it was hard to imagine one without the other. They thought the same and shared the same values. Together they were so strong; one would have been completely lost without the other. They were together and we were together.

Their influence gave us the strength to carry on and we believed they were looking over us somewhere and guiding us, even though we were never a particularly religious family. We didn't go to church on a regular basis. We had been baptized and we were made to go to Sunday School a bit when we were little. My sister also had a Holy Communion. We were interested in religion but we didn't practise it. Mum was very spiritual and both she and Dad were open-minded about all faiths; that was one of reasons they loved India so much.

They were brought back from Sri Lanka and the funeral was arranged. There had already been a few brief newspaper reports when news leaked out that they were missing, some of which gave our names and ages and said that it was believed we had been orphaned. When their deaths were confirmed, there was renewed interest. The police were concerned that the funeral, which was to be held in the small Hampshire town of Blackwater near Marie's house, would attract a lot of media interest. We were taken there in unmarked police cars with blacked-out windows. It was, of course, a very difficult day for everyone. All our relatives were there and were all as upset as we were, but we'd resolved to have a celebration of their lives, rather than a memorial to their deaths. We knew that's what Mum and Dad would have wanted. They were so full of life, they would not have wanted to see anyone saddened by their passing. I can remember the day in snatches. No one was allowed to wear black. There were throngs of people. In the end we reckoned around 500 people turned up.

There was laughter as well as tears. One of the songs played was 'Always Look On The Bright Side of Life' by Monty Python. It was hard not to smile when that came on. It was one of Dad's favourite songs and in a comic way seemed to sum up his attitude to life and the attitude he would have had to his own funeral. He would have enjoyed the fact that people were laughing.

There were so many people, I didn't get to see everyone. In part I think my mind shut a lot out. For months after, people spoke to me and told me they were there but I couldn't remember them.

Marie did a reading. She read the famous poem 'Footprints in the Sand'. The verse is about someone depicting their life as a journey portrayed by footsteps on a beach and it was particularly poignant.

I gave a eulogy, on behalf of all of us. I thanked our parents for our upbringing and for broadening our horizons by taking us travelling. I thanked them for the opportunities they had given us.

'They will always be a few steps behind us, watching over us and making sure we always do the right thing,' I concluded.

I managed to get through the speech without breaking down and when I got home, I folded it up and locked it away. I've only looked at it once or twice in the last ten years. I was in my own space that day. I had friends there to support me and also people I hadn't seen in years, so it was a hectic day. It passed in a haze and, since then, I've deliberately blanked it out. Later in the afternoon, after our parents were cremated, I got quite drunk. It was the only way I could get through the rest of the day. I just wanted to forget that part of what had happened to us and remember Mum and Dad as the wonderful, positive people they were. All of us wanted that; we've never had much time for negativity. We have our parents to thank for that.

A few days after the funeral, when we were still reeling from the events of the previous months, it was Rosie's tenth birthday.

We tried as hard as we could to give her a fun day, but no one felt much like celebrating. Her birthday also coincided with Mother's Day and St Patrick's Day, which we'd always celebrated because of Dad's Irish roots. It would normally have been a time of celebration and joy. Instead, those special days just emphasized the hole that had been left in our lives. Years later and we still tend to avoid marking certain times of year. Rather than celebrate we just carry on as normal. Many of the happy events in the calendar have been overshadowed by what happened. For the same reason, we tend not to celebrate Christmas too much either.

The funeral allowed some closure and the opportunity to start to move on. All the while there was a chance Mum and Dad were alive somewhere, our stay at Marie's was temporary. After the confirmation of their deaths, it was permanent. Marie and Liam never hesitated in offering us their home. They consulted with me and they sat the younger ones down and asked us where we wanted to go.

'Is there anywhere else you want to live or anyone else you want to live with? Are you happy with us as your guardians?'

We all agreed.

'I'm going to look into adoption,' she continued. 'It makes sense if I become your legal guardian.'

I was the exception. I was nearing my eighteenth birthday so, by the time the paperwork went through, it would not have been worth it in my case.

Unfortunately, however, it was not as simple as that for the others. As if the stress of losing our parents was not enough, questions were asked about Marie's suitability as an adoptive parent. The social services, who were taking an increased interest in us, felt Marie was too young to look after a ten-year-old, a twelve-year-old and a fifteen-year-old, even though she had taken control from the minute we got back and had looked after us ably through the difficult months since. They also questioned the suitability of the house.

Social workers would turn up at the house regularly to assess her and to check up on us and our progress. She spoke to me often about it. I knew the best place for all of us was together and couldn't countenance the idea of us being split up. The social workers had little idea or understanding of just how strong, independent and resilient we all were. No one really knew apart from us. Even older relatives wondered if Marie and Liam, who was a bit older, would cope. We found ourselves having to check in and tell the social workers where we were going and what we were doing. It wasn't easy. Marie felt there were a lot of people meddling in our family business. She was under enough pressure without the extra stress. There were so many other issues going on in my head, it didn't register with me quite what Marie was having to put up with. It must have been awful for her.

In the end, several things happened which finally allowed her to adopt the other children. Firstly she hired a lawyer to fight to keep us together. Then she got planning permission and the funds to build an extension on the house so that she could create another bedroom for Paul and me. By that point Marie had had to sacrifice her full-time job and career to become a carer to Mattie and Rosie, which meant a loss of much-needed money. Neither Liam nor Marie mentioned it directly, but again they alluded to the fact that help had been given and it was obvious that money was coming from somewhere to pay the lawyers and the builders. It was as if someone was looking out for us all.

By the time everything had been finalized, it was summer 2005. After the funeral I lived in Marie's house for a month or so but I soon realized just how cramped it would be. I needed my own space and I also had to start thinking about earning a living. At seventeen I had no problems with moving out and getting on with my life. We still had the caravan in the New Forest and I went down there and got my old lifeguarding job back. I stayed for the summer and tried to fill my days with activity to keep my mind occupied. I was totally self-sufficient and independent and I enjoyed it. I could cook but instead I just grabbed easy-to-prepare food. It became a running joke that I managed to live off Golden Grahams cereal. I didn't have any career plans. I had planned to work with Dad on his website, but I couldn't bring myself to resurrect that idea. Instead I worked all the hours I could. Most days I did double shifts and filled in for people who were on holiday. As it was the summer, it was a good time to pick up extra work.

On many occasions it all became too much. I'd try my best to divert myself. If I wasn't working I'd go out and do something; I'd play golf, cricket and football. I partied hard on occasions when I went out with friends to Bournemouth and the coast. There were times when I let loose and wanted to forget what was going on.

Marie kept an eye on me and, one week, when I ended up doing about ninety hours, she spoke to the people at the leisure centre and told them off for letting me work so much. She was a protective big sis.

My other siblings were enrolled in new schools, but it took time. Paul hated it. It had been a long time since he'd attended school and he was mature beyond his years and didn't see the point in going.

A few months after the funeral, as we were mourning and beginning to find our way through life without Mum and Dad, the family was hit by another hammer blow. Dad's mum, Mary, our nan, died. She had been frail since Dad went missing and was devastated at losing her son. There is no doubt the shock and grief killed her. Once again we had another funeral to arrange. Nan had been a big part of our lives when we were growing up and we missed her dearly. The tsunami had claimed another member of our family.

There were times over those early months when we all wondered if we'd ever be able to enjoy life again. The weeks after Mum and Dad's funeral were particularly dark. One thing shone through, however: hope. I was never in doubt that life would get better and no matter how low I felt, I always knew that in the scheme of things I had been lucky. I had somewhere to live. I had a job and food to eat. I wasn't living in a slum in Mumbai or begging on the streets of Delhi. I'd seen enough of the world to know that I was privileged. Paul felt the same way. Thanks to our parents and the global perspective they had given us, we were able to have hope and remain positive.

Little glimmers of light did start to show through. There was not much laughter to begin with and when one of us did find ourselves laughing at something, we would feel guilty. Of course it was irrational. The last thing our parents would have wanted was for us to be miserable. They did everything in their power when they were alive to make sure we had happy, carefree, fulfilled lives.

I can pinpoint certain times when we started to turn corners. Towards the end of the football season in spring 2005 we were invited to go and watch a game of football at QPR. Dad had been a huge fan of the club and so were Paul and I. A family friend knew someone who worked at the ground in west London and they arranged for us to have a box and to meet the manager and some of the players. We got the full VIP treatment. We invited some family and friends and, at first, it felt awkward. Dad was very noticeable in his absence. He should have been there. He would have loved to have been there.

It was quiet in the box as we waited for the game to start.

And then someone made a comment that made us all laugh.

'Your old man supported this club all his life and he never managed to get a box. He'll be gutted he missed out!'

It broke the ice and, as the day went on, people relaxed and the banter started. It was like the good old days again.

Other things started to happen. In August I turned eighteen. I thought it would be a muted affair, perhaps a meal out with my brothers and sisters. But I was taken to the cricket club in New Milton and when I walked into the lounge it was full of people. My sisters and my mates had organized a surprise party. It was a good night and another example of how life had started to move on. We'd all started living again.

Later that summer I went away to Crete on my first lads' holiday. It wasn't the type of travelling I'd been used to but it was cool. It was fun and carefree.

Christmas came and went. The first anniversary of the tsunami was hard, but we got through it.

Paul, Rosie and Mattie settled into life with Marie. She was a strong and able parent figure. What she said went. She'd postponed her wedding for a year and had begun to think again about what she was going to do. Her original plan had been to have a big white wedding in the UK with all the family and friends present. Mum had made Rosie's bridesmaid dress, which was hanging in a wardrobe in Marie's house. Dad was going to give Marie away.

But those original plans didn't seem right after everything that had happened and Marie had a rethink. She wanted a smaller affair and decided to get married in Sorrento in Italy instead, with fifteen close friends and family.

Rosie was still a bridesmaid and wore the dress Mum made. She looked beautiful, as did Marie. The ceremony was conducted at an open-air altar on a cliff top overlooking the sea. We all felt our parents there watching. Paul and I walked our sister down the aisle. It was an emotional day for everyone, but it ended up being an incredible one. It was very happy and very funny. It was like our family used to be. We all had a laugh together. After the ceremony we walked down the main street in Sorrento to the restaurant we'd booked for the meal after the wedding. We stopped the traffic; it backed up behind us and drivers tooted and cheered. It was hot, sunny and beautiful. We thought about Mum and Dad and spoke about them. We knew they were not there in person but we were not grieving; we remembered them in a happy way and that in turn made us feel that life could go on without them. Their absence was felt, but there was no mourning. It was a celebration.

None of us will ever forget our parents and some days it's hard. Sometimes things happen that remind you of what you've lost.

Each of us dealt with our loss differently. Mattie and Jo struggled sometimes. Rosie was always a fighter and Paul and I tried as best we could to remain positive. Marie was the sensible one and filled Mum's shoes.

People often want to know how we coped in the immediate aftermath of the tsunami and how we managed to move on. I've always felt that our parents have been there all along. The skills and maturity they gave us guided us. For me, after the wave hit, I felt that all the training, skills and knowledge that Mum and Dad gave us over the years kicked in. It was almost as if Dad was there. I didn't need to ask what to do, I just knew.

Our parents were gone; lost to the sea. But their spirit and the things they taught us remained and helped us cope in the situation we found ourselves in. They'd always encouraged us to be adventurous, self-sufficient, questioning, business-minded and positive. Imbued with these qualities, it wasn't long before I started to get itchy feet again. The urge to travel was in my blood, just as it had been in my father's. I started to think about what I wanted to do with my life and although I'd never had any career plans, I knew I wanted to make some money and I wanted to see the places I'd not had a chance to see with my parents.

CHAPTER 13

Moving On

WORKING AS A lifeguard was never going to be a long-term career plan. It was a great job. I blew my whistle, sat on a high chair and generally had a laugh. Everyone I worked with was young and up for fun. They all played sports as well, so after work we'd get together and have games of squash or badminton. It was good fun, but I knew I needed to look for longer-term work and at the end of the summer we sold the caravan and I moved back into Marie's house.

I wasn't sure what I wanted to do, but I wanted to get some experience in an office-based environment. I needed to get a career. My CV had several holes in it. I had two qualifications and I'd been travelling, but I wrote out a CV and massaged the truth a little, claiming that I'd worked in sales and marketing in my dad's fashion business. I put my details on a website called CV Library. Entrepreneurs were still getting to grips with the possibilities of the Internet at that stage and the site was a database where companies could pay to search for prospective employees. It was a good idea; most people still relied on recruitment agencies or newspapers to look for vacancies.

A few days passed and I received a call.

'My name's Lee,' said a cheerful voice. 'I'm one of the founders of CV Library. I've been looking at your CV. You're young and ambitious. We may have an opportunity.'

I was interested in hearing what Lee had to offer.

'Can you give me some details?' I asked.

'Why don't you come in and have a chat?'

So I did.

Marie drove me to their office, which was just a couple of miles from her house in a village called Church Crookham. They were based in a converted barn and the village was in the middle of nowhere. I wore a suit. When I walked in, Lee, who was in his early twenties, shook my hand and showed me to a seat.

'Nice suit,' he remarked. I wasn't convinced he was being serious.

There was another guy there: Brian. He explained he ran the techie side of the business and Lee ran the sales and marketing.

They cut to the chase.

'We're actually looking for someone young to come and work with us. It's a new business with a lot of potential. We want someone to help us in sales,' explained Lee. 'We noticed that you live nearby.'

I liked Lee and Brian from the start. Having seen how my dad took ideas and developed them into businesses, I had every respect for what they were doing. They told me their story.

Lee had worked in a couple of recruitment agencies and came up with the idea for an Internet-based job board. A lot of people had shot down the idea, believing that people would always rely on recruitment agencies and newspaper ads and that the Internet would never be big enough to challenge that. But Lee realized there was potential and asked his mates if any of them knew a computer programmer. Brian was recommended. He was a BT engineer, but had a big interest in the Internet. The screens on his desk looked like something from the *Matrix* movies. He could hack into anything and was well ahead of his time in terms of computer technology.

Lee and Brian met in the local pub and discussed the idea. They sketched ideas on the back of a beer mat. They were both young and started off working out of their bedrooms. When the site was launched, it started to make money and finally they moved into the barn. Lee's father's carpet business was next door and Lee worked with him as a carpet fitter while he also built up his company. That was how he could afford to employ a salesman.

Their first-ever client was the BBC and they were tasked with finding six blonde and six brunette models from the database they held. Brian took the order. The person who placed it asked, 'And does your database include details about hair colour?' It didn't, of course, but the lads blagged it and Brian rang around people listed on the site to ask them their hair colour. From those humble roots the company has now grown into one of the most successful online recruitment businesses. It holds the details of several million jobseekers and all the biggest companies use it.

They asked me about myself. I lied and told them I had experience in sales and customer services. I told them I did lifeguarding and that I'd been travelling. Lee liked that because he had been to India. I didn't tell them about the tsunami.

Initially, they sold ads on the site to fund it, but had wondered what would happen if they brought someone in to sell it actively to clients. That was my role. They offered me the job there and then. There were just the three of us at the start and it felt exciting to be at the beginning of something. I accepted the offer; the wage was around £12,000 a year with commission.

I started a few days later, initially selling ads for £49. I had no sales training. On my first day, Lee dumped a copy of the Yellow Pages phone directory and a phone on my desk and told me to start selling. I didn't have a script, my patter was all off the top of my head. At first, recruitment firms didn't get it. The idea was new, but when I explained the potential of the Internet they started to understand and realized that paper CVs would eventually become a thing of the past as the world became more and more connected and people relied more on email and Internet communication.

CV Library grew and grew. More staff were employed. In the early days it was basic. My job was fluid. One week I painted the offices with Lee and Brian. We had no electronic accounts system. I'd write down who I sold to and Lee invoiced them or we took payments over the phone.

There were times when I'd get a deal for £800 and Lee and Brian would be whooping and high-fiving. We could get quite carried away with ourselves.

'Come on, Rob, you've got one more in you,' Lee would urge. Then we'd go down the pub to celebrate.

He pushed me as hard as he could; he was harsh but fair. Lots of people came and went because they couldn't hack the pressure, but I loved it and we became good friends, socializing after work.

Marie was strict about me coming in late at night, so I'd often stay at Lee's if we'd been out on a particularly late night.

I used to ride to the office on my bike in the snow and rain, setting out early in the morning. I got changed into my workwear when I was there and stayed late, often working until seven or eight at night.

Although it was challenging work, we had a good laugh. As we were all young, there were plenty of practical jokes.

Lee had a strange habit of always insisting on writing with a pencil and I'd deliberately snap the lead in the pencils in the office so he could never find one to use.

He once went on holiday and, for reasons I've forgotten, one of the girls who was working there at the time needed to go into the loft. We told her only to walk on the beams and not to step on the insulation. She didn't listen, however, and put her foot straight through the ceiling, leaving a huge hole. I took a picture and sent it to Lee.

'Don't worry, mate, sales are going through the roof,' I wrote on the caption.

Lee always went away at Christmas and one year, a day before he left, I asked, 'When do you want to hand over presents?'

Lee panicked. He assumed I'd bought him something and didn't want the embarrassment of not reciprocating, so made an excuse and left for an hour. When he came back, he came over to my desk with a bag of presents.

'Happy Christmas,' he said, handing them over.

'Thanks, mate,' I said. He waited awkwardly.

'I haven't got you anything,' I shrugged.

We became good friends. Most weekends I would end up going to Bournemouth where I knew more people. I didn't have many friends around where I lived in Farnborough as I'd only ended up there after Sri Lanka. Lee noticed and would invite me along when he went out with his mates. He also knew the manager of the local football team and got me in to play for them. He never asked too many questions, but he realized there was something unusual about my domestic situation. I lived with my sister and didn't talk about my parents.

I told him about the tsunami and being orphaned after I'd been working for him for about six months. We were chatting about our backgrounds and he asked what my parents did. I never avoided the issue; I didn't offer it up though because, in the past, it had made people react to me differently. I didn't want people to treat me any differently and I certainly didn't want pity. Lee was just the same after he knew as he was before.

I worked for him for over a year. I learned loads about negotiation, marketing and online business. I enjoyed it immensely, but I always harboured an ambition to carry on travelling. I had always wanted to carry on with the journey I set out on with my parents in 2001. Our parents had talked about seeing Australia and New Zealand and I wanted to go there. It was unfinished business. I needed to get it out of my system. I liked working but I wanted to see the world. There is so much to see and, if you don't, you have led a sheltered life. Why would you not want to go out and experience different places, people and cultures?

At nineteen, I'd saved enough and I couldn't resist the urge any longer. I handed in my notice. Lee told me I could go back whenever I wanted. I bought a £1,000 round-the-world ticket from STA Travel which had twelve stops and planned a route.

Paul was training to be a plumber at college at the time and envious. He was seventeen and would have loved to have joined me. He had to wait another two years before he set off travelling again. Marie was right behind my decision. Besides, she had a houseful and one less person would free up valuable space in her home.

The first place I went to was India. I wanted to go back there and see a bit more of it. I went to Delhi, Agra, Mumbai, Kerala, Goa and Rajasthan.

Initially, I planned to go back to some of the places we'd stayed in as a family and in Goa I went back to the complex where we rented our villa. It was full of good memories so at first I felt drawn there. I was on my own and I wanted to go there because it was familiar. But it just didn't feel right being there alone. It was so different from what it had been before. The place itself had changed: it was busier and more commercial but it seemed empty without my parents.

The owners were pleased to see me and remembered me. They asked what had happened to us and asked how Mum and Dad were. I told them the story and they were devastated. Everything seemed raw as I explained. It was hard to talk about it and then it was uncomfortable being around them. They didn't know what to say.

I was planning to stay at the complex longer, but I got out. It had lost its soul. I met Jeedi the jeweller and had to tell him what had happened to our family. There was a local hotel owner we knew who I visited. When he heard my news he offered me a room and a meal whenever I wanted, but I didn't end up going back because it felt awkward. Instead I stayed somewhere else and avoided places I'd been to with Mum and Dad.

Afterwards I felt lonely. It hit me that I was on my own and the absence of Mum and Dad was palpable. I headed away to a different part of the country.

It took time to get used to being a lone traveller, but there is a community on the road and in most places I stayed I found people to talk to and share experiences with.

I'd never shied away from making new friends. The independence we'd been allowed as kids gave me confidence which helped me. One night I was by myself in a restaurant and started chatting to two guys. We met at the urinal and they asked me where I was from in the UK. Matt and Louis were from Essex and about ten years older than me. They were a good laugh and we ended up travelling together for several months. They were following a similar itinerary to me and planned to see the same places so we arranged to stick together. It was common practice when travelling to hook up with other people and as I saw and experienced new places, the ghosts of the past weighed less heavily on me.

As a group of mates, we did what travellers do. We messed around, we got drunk occasionally and we got tattoos. I got a Buddha tattoo on my arm and an angel on my back which took four hours to finish. I chose Buddha because of the statue I used to divert Mattie's attention when we were walking along the train track after the tsunami in Weligama. It also epitomized the idea that we are all part of the universe. I drew the angel design myself. The figure was half man and half woman to signify Mum and Dad and the sacrifices they made for us. I had the date of the tsunami tattooed in it too. I had my tattoos done in a clean, modern place. Louis got his done by a bloke in a market who had his machinery hooked up to a battery which kept running out. Louis asked for his name in Hindi. Afterwards he noticed locals kept calling him Lewis and realized the tattooist had spelled the name wrong!

I met loads of diverse people. I fell for a girl from the UK who was at the end of her trip and almost went back home with her. I'd been travelling and living at my sister's for most of my teenage life and so hadn't had much chance to meet girls. She was the first girl I was serious about and it was cool. I spoke to friends back home and told them I was thinking of going back. They, along with Matt and Louis, convinced me not to.

'Don't fall at the first hurdle,' was their big-brotherly advice. I'm glad I listened to them. The year I spent travelling was amazing.

Before we left India, I fell ill. In all my years travelling, I'd never been troubled by illness but my luck ran out when we were staying in some beach shacks in a town in the south of the country. I have no idea what caused it – whether I ate something or caught a bug – but I started to get stomach cramps and felt light-headed. Within an hour I was burning up with a temperature, shivering, sweating and feeling faint. It was terrifying. Matt and Louis had gone off somewhere and I knew I needed to get to a hospital. I staggered through the town until I found a taxi to take me to the nearest clinic, where I was admitted. Thankfully I had travel insurance and so was treated in a private room. By the time I arrived, I was delirious. I was hooked up on a drip and spent a couple of days fading in and out of sleep while whatever it was ran its course through my guts. At some point, while I was in there, someone robbed my money.

Being older, Matt and Louis felt a duty of care towards me and when they realized I'd disappeared, went looking for me. They checked with the police and came to the hospital where they found me recovering and took the piss. When I was discharged, I was given tablets to take.

We planned to head to Thailand so we could go to the famous New Year's Eve party on the beach at a place called Koh Pangang and headed to Mumbai to catch a flight there. I started taking the tablets I'd been given after leaving hospital. After taking the first one I suffered some form of allergic reaction. My tongue started to swell and I had trouble breathing. I had to go back into hospital for an adrenaline shot.

Eventually we got to Thailand. It was a place I'd never been to and so it was a completely fresh experience. I loved it. It was new, crazy and exotic. We stayed in Bangkok for a while. We went to a Thai kick-boxing match, I got propositioned by a ladyboy and we enjoyed some of the more unusual sights and sounds of the city.

We headed down to the coast for Christmas and New Year's Eve. One of the places we visited, Phi Phi, had been damaged in the tsunami and parts of it were still in ruins. Outside of Sri Lanka, it was the first place I'd been where the wave had caused havoc. It was a difficult place to be at a difficult time of year and the sound of the sea spooked me at night. We moved on and went island-hopping along the coast.

On Boxing Day I was on the beach. I'd had a few beers and emotions got the better of me. It was always going to be a hard day and the location didn't help. I told the guys what had happened to me. By then I was good mates with them and after I told them they didn't treat me any differently, they still took the mickey and bantered.

I was always a bit conscious of being by the sea, especially at night when we stayed in shacks and treehouses. But I started to realize that what had happened was a one-off and that I couldn't live in fear and stop experiencing new things because of it. The odds of it happening again were massive. If you fall off a bike you don't stop riding it, you get back on.

From Thailand my travels continued through South-East Asia. We took the train to Laos and a place called Vang Vieng: a town on the Nam Song River which was a magnet for young travellers. The main street was lined with restaurants and bars and there were plenty of cheap guest houses to stay in. The must-do activity was tubing: floating down the river on a big rubber inner-tube and stopping off along the way to enjoy some of the bars that lined the riverbanks. It was a waterborne pub crawl and attracted thousands of young people a year. Along the way there were rope swings and zip wires which crossed the water. At stages the banks turned into cliffs which towered 40 feet above. People would take zip wires from the top. The mix of cheap alcohol and adventure sports proved fatal on many occasions. Everyone was out to get drunk. It was the most dangerous bar-hopping route in the world. When I was there, a Japanese girl missed when she went to grab a zip wire and tumbled 40 feet into the water below. The crowd that was watching went deadly quiet as she hit the water with a sickening splat. After what seemed like an age, she spluttered to the surface and everyone cheered as people dived in to help her out the water.

The weeks passed quickly and were full of new experiences and places. I could almost feel my horizons expanding. Even on the days where there were no activities planned, I just enjoyed the excitement of being somewhere different. I often thought of my parents and how they would have loved to have seen the places I was seeing.

After Thailand, Louis, Matt and I went our separate ways. I went to Singapore and Bali. Louis continued round Asia and Matt went to Australia.

Bali was unreal. I met some great people. I met a Czech guy who could speak nine languages. I met doctors and bricklayers. I realized how constraining life in Farnborough had been. Being out in the world reminded me how weird and wonderful people are.

I met people from all over the world and from all backgrounds. I hung out with a mad group of Finnish guys and we jumped off a hotel roof into a pool. We went surfing at 5 a.m. after a big night out. We played stupid games, dared each other to get more tattoos and met some great girls.

Certain moments always stick out. I remember one night I was in a room with two Swedish girls. Being Swedes, they were quite comfortable with nudity and had liberal attitudes. They were topless with just bikini bottoms on. I was sitting on my own with them watching a DVD. They were gorgeous. I was nineteen. I thought to myself, 'None of my friends back home are ever going to believe this if I tell them.'

In Bali I hooked up with a crazy Kiwi surfer called Zeek and we had a brush with the law. Bali is a conservative Muslim country and while the rules are relaxed and tourists are well looked after, the police like to keep young travellers in check. They don't want to hear that you are bumming your way around the world. They want to hear that you are in education and training for a career. Some of them are also inclined to ask for spurious payments if they pull you over, as happened when Zeek and I hired a couple of mopeds. We'd heard about the police habit of eliciting bribes and so when we saw a police checkpoint up ahead on a quiet road, we made a sharp turn to try and avoid it. Unfortunately the road we turned into was a dead end and the officers noticed our suspicious behaviour and a couple of them sped after us on powerful motorbikes.

We were cornered.

'Is there a problem, officers?' I asked, getting off my bike and trying to look casual. We hadn't actually done anything wrong but, as is often the case when you are young and you get pulled over by the police, I felt guilty.

'Why didn't you stop?' asked one of the serious-looking cops.

'I didn't see you,' I replied.

'Papers, please,' the man said, holding out his hand.

I handed it over. He leafed through it while the other officer questioned Zeek, who looked like a typical surf hippy with long, unwashed blond hair.

'What is the purpose of your visit to Bali,' he demanded.

'Well, dude, I'm studying to be a surgeon and I'm over here to visit some of the cultural sites on the island.'

The cop looked us both up and down and raised a cynical eyebrow.

'I'm fining you for not stopping and for not wearing helmets,' one said. Then he asked for the equivalent of around £50 in

Indonesian Rupiah. I was living off £20 a day, I'd saved hard for the funds and wanted my money to last as long as it possibly could. I felt I had no option but to bluff rather than hand over cash to a corrupt policeman.

'Can you write out a ticket then?'

I could see the officer flinch slightly. He was used to people handing over their cash and putting it down to one of the inconveniences of travelling.

He looked me in the eye.

'And what is the purpose of your visit?' he said.

'I'm on holiday before I go back to the UK and begin work as a policeman,' I said. 'My dad is a policeman in London.'

The man scoffed.

'Call Scotland Yard and ask for him, he'll sort out the ticket,' I bluffed.

The cop looked at his partner. They obviously realized we were on to their scheme. Thankfully, rather than get nasty, they decided it wasn't worth the effort to pursue their scheme.

'On this occasion we'll let you off but don't let us see you without helmets again,' he said. They got on their bikes and rode off empty-handed.

I stayed in Bali a couple of weeks longer than I planned, mainly because of a lovely Swedish girl I met. When she moved on, I went to Australia where I stayed in Sydney and Melbourne and travelled up to the Gold Coast. I met a mate from college who was over there working as a tennis coach and spent a few months with him.

I stayed with my Uncle John and Aunt Anne in Brisbane. They had never heard the full story of what happened on Boxing Day from any of us and none of Dad's other siblings had told them. No one talked about it. It was eating them up, they couldn't come to terms with it and one night, as we sat outside enjoying a drink in the warm night air, they asked me about it. I told them what I knew. I told them what had happened to us, that Mum and Dad had died saving Mattie and Rosie. I explained how we managed to get back to Colombo and get home. It was emotional, but I was now at ease talking about it. If they had asked me six months earlier, I would have clammed up to protect myself. Travelling had helped me clear a lot of things in my mind. They thanked me for letting them know. Hopefully it helped them move on too.

From Australia I went to Fiji, where I played rugby on the beach and went island-hopping. I then headed to Hawaii, Los Angeles and New York. All the way round the globe, I used Internet cafes to keep in touch with my brothers and sisters. I'd set up my very first Facebook account in an Internet cafe in India and updated that whenever I got the chance and also used it to keep up to date with news from home. While I was away, I got the news that Marie was pregnant and, by the time I got back, I had a nephew, Kieron, to meet.

Paul was finishing college and was struggling to find work. I spoke to him regularly and he sounded disaffected. He'd hated school but had always been a hard worker. No one was giving him the chance. There were no opportunities for trainee plumbers because tradesmen were wary of taking on apprentices in case they eventually undercut them and stole their business.

Mattie and Rosie were still at school and seemed to be doing OK. Rosie had developed a real love of music and was also becoming a proficient footballer. She had trials for England at school level and was also approached by a couple of club sides. She was outgoing and a bit of a character. You always knew when Rosie was around. She's coped very well in the years after our parents' death.

As I made my way through America, I felt like I was on the home run and began to look forward to getting back home. It was weird being back in the Western world after my experiences in India and Asia. It became expensive as I reached the US. LA was hard to backpack in. Not much is cheap there. I was so used to minimal living and suddenly I was back in a modern city. It was as if I was spinning back into Western civilization.

By the time I got to New York, I was out of money and although it was a great city, by then I wanted to get home. I'd missed home and family and I wanted to see Kieron and my mates.

I came back to the UK skint, with no plans but with a lot of amazing memories. I had some incredible experiences and met amazing people. Some places moved me to tears. I'll always remember the eerie and moving feeling I got when I visited the memorial to the victims of the Bali bombings and the Pearl Harbor memorial. I spent time at both, trying to piece together my traumatic experiences, and I thought harder about the people involved in those events because I understood a little of what the people caught up in those tragedies may have felt.

It was late summer when my round-the-world trip ended. I'd grown up, I'd become more confident, and I'd come to terms with some of the issues that were troubling me. I had needed to go away to get my head straight. It felt like a chapter had been closed; an urge had been put to bed. I'd journeyed on my own but my parents were with me and I'd seen the things they had wanted to see. It felt right.

It was good to see everyone. Marie picked me up from the airport and we went and had a meal together. It was great to meet my new nephew and to catch up with everyone. I'd been away for a year and they hadn't changed but I had. I wanted more out of life. I hadn't considered the future before because I was too intent on living in the here and now while I was travelling with Mum and Dad and after the tsunami it was all I could do to deal with the present.

But I knew I wanted to do something in life that would allow me to keep having new experiences and learn new things. I didn't want that one trip to be it. I wanted to go back out in the world and I also wanted to be involved in something that would help others. I just didn't know what that would be.

CHAPTER 14

Hey, Jute

WHEN I RETURNED Lee offered me my job back at CV Library but I wanted to move on and try something new. A friend I knew was moving out of his place and looking for someone to share a place with in Bournemouth. I knew a lot of people in the town and moved in with him. I found a job in a recruitment company there called Platinum. It was a young business which specialized in finding top-end chefs for restaurants and hotels and was run by three guys: Neil, Paul and Simon.

The interview was tough, but after they'd grilled me the four of us went to play crazy golf, then to McDonald's and then to the pub. It was my kind of business. I like unorthodox people.

While I was living in Bournemouth, I also met a girl. We were together for a year but she had always wanted to go travelling and I'd only just returned. Although I wanted to do more, I wasn't ready to pack up and disappear again yet and so she went on her own.

I did well at the recruitment firm and enjoyed the work. I got to visit top restaurants and hotels all over the country and the guys I worked with taught me a lot. Lee and I remained good friends and he kept an eye on my progress. He often reiterated his offer and, a year after I started at Platinum, he tried to entice me back again. CV Library had continued to grow and was doing well. Lots of online businesses struggled to find ways to make decent money, but Lee's had and he wanted to expand the corporate side of his site, which had the potential to grow even more as the recruitment industry increasingly migrated online. CV Library had the advantage of being one of the early online recruitment pioneers and had been built into a strong, established brand. Lee asked me to go back and set up and run a new department selling to big corporate clients. I liked the idea of taking on the challenge of being there at the start of something new. I accepted his offer and moved to Church Crookham, where CV Library was still based. I rented a bungalow there with another mate, Andy.

Life was good. I worked long, hard hours, made good money, had a decent car, few responsibilities and a comfortable life. We had some cool parties at the bungalow. One New Year's we recreated the Koh Pangang beach party in the back garden. Everyone wore beachwear, some came in wetsuits and we strung the place with fairy lights and even managed to get hold of some palm trees.

Meanwhile, Paul was having less luck. He was fed up. He'd turned nineteen and struggled to find work. Instead of plumbing, he got a job working in B&Q where he'd often work double shifts all week. It annoyed me that someone with obvious talents who was not work-shy struggled to find work mainly because the school system didn't suit him. Paul had always wanted to go travelling and he saved hard to make the dream become reality. As soon as he had enough, he booked his ticket and flew off. He took a similar route to the one I had taken and also went to New Zealand.

After a year he returned, but it didn't take him long to realize that there was nothing in the UK for him. After a couple of months, struggling to find work again, he realized he'd be better off in Australia where the climate was better and there were more opportunities. He got back on a plane and ended up living in Melbourne, where he stayed for two years. I respected his decision. Initially he bummed around and did some temp work, then he got a job in a warehouse, worked his way up into the office, was given a role in sales and eventually became an account manager with a car and a salary quadruple what he'd have been earning in the UK. He had to travel to the opposite side of the world before someone realized his potential. The money he earned also went a lot further in Australia, so he had a good standard of living.

Periodically, Paul came back to the UK to visit. Usually when he did, it involved a few nights out. On one particular night things got a little out of hand.

The day started normally enough. Paul was with one of his friends and we were planning where to go. He was due to fly back to Australia in a few days and we wanted one last big night out.

'Why don't we go somewhere new and different?' he said. So we went to Southampton: a seaside town on the south coast. We decided to stay the night and booked into a hotel where we left our car and headed out. We did the usual: we went to a few bars, we went to a club where beer was being sold for £1 a bottle, we went to a casino and finally we ended up in the only bar we could find that was open. It was a heavy night and Paul's mate started chatting up some of the girls who worked in the bar. In the early hours of the morning, he invited one back to the hotel. She was still working but said she'd go after she finished. He gave her the room number and said he'd leave the door open for her.

When we got back to the hotel, the messing around continued and eventually I went to my room and left Paul and his mate to it in the room they were sharing.

The next morning we all awoke with hangovers, but Paul and his mate had a bigger problem. Their wallets were gone. They'd left the door open and while they were passed out someone, presumably the girl from the club, had come along and helped herself. It was all quite predictable and an inconvenience, but not the end of the world. All they had to do was make a few calls, cancel their cards and order new ones and the problem would be solved and lessons learned.

However, soon after we all surfaced and realized what had happened, Paul got a call on his phone. The number was withheld. He answered it.

'I've got your wallets. If you want them back you need to pay. If you don't, I'll be telling everyone you know about the type of places you hang out in and the kind of company you keep,' said a gruff male voice. Presumably he meant the bar and the girl who worked there.

'I want five hundred pounds from each of you. If you go to the police I'll stitch you up.'

Initially Paul laughed, thinking it was a wind-up.

'Do what you want, mate, I'm going to Australia tomorrow, it doesn't bother me,' he said.

But then things took a disturbing turn.

'I've got your driving licence and I know where you live. I also know where your family are. You wouldn't want anything to happen to them like it did to your parents, would you?' the man growled.

The guy had Googled Paul's name and seen a news item posted on the BBC website soon after the tsunami which listed the UK victims and gave brief details about each. It reported that Mum and Dad had left six children and gave our names and ages. The guy had worked out who Paul was and he was threatening the rest of our family.

We didn't know what to do.

'Look, we'll give you a couple of hundred quid but that's all we've got,' offered Paul. But the man was not backing down and continued his threats. In the end he told us to think about it and that he'd call back to discuss where we were to drop off the money.

We went to the police straight away. We had nothing to hide and there was no way I was taking a risk by trying to deal with him. The police told us we had become the victims of a fairly common and nasty scam that had been happening in the town for quite a while. The threats of violence towards our family concerned them greatly. They believed there was a network of crooks operating around the town's clubs and they explained that we could hopefully help apprehend them.

As the oldest, I was nominated as the main contact point when the man called back and I spent time being briefed by the police. They wanted us to run with the scam and to arrange to meet the man and hand over money. It would be a sting operation. Cops would be watching and I'd be accompanied by a specially trained officer. It was all explained in detail.

'You won't be in any danger,' they reassured us. 'These are nasty people and they need to be caught. You are the best chance we have.'

I was coached as to what to say when he called. I needed to draw him into conversation and get him to admit he had threatened to kill my family and that he was blackmailing me. The call would be taped.

When the phone rang later that Sunday afternoon, I was sitting in a room in Southampton police station, surrounded by officers.

I answered.

'This is Rob, Paul's older brother,' I said. 'Why are you doing this, we're just a couple of young blokes. We're not hurting anyone.'

'Don't dick me around,' the man snarled. 'I told your brother. I want one thousand pounds cash and your family lives.'

'Why would you want to hurt them? They haven't done anything to you. Why are you blackmailing my brother?'

'Because I can,' he laughed.

I'd been told to agree to meet him in public and to tell him that I was not going to meet him alone.

'How do I know you'll leave us alone if I do what you say?'

'Trust me,' he sneered.

'OK. But we meet in a public place and I'm bringing a mate,' I said.

He agreed.

'Meet me in Pizza Hut in Basingstoke shopping centre tomorrow at midday. Don't try anything silly. I'll be watching.'

My heart was pounding when he hung up.

I'd been in some surreal situations in my life but this was one of the strangest. It was like I was in the middle of a Hollywood movie. The next day I was picked up by the police and taken to a station in Hampshire where I met the undercover officer who was posing as my friend for the money drop.

He was in his thirties, not particularly tall or bulky and looked totally unassuming.

'Is he going to be all right if things get tricky?' I asked an officer, pointing at my partner.

He laughed.

'That bloke is the best there is. He's trained in close protection, firearms, self-defence, everything. Trust me, he's not going to let anything happen to you.'

The man introduced himself. Let's call him Dave; he probably didn't give me his real name anyway! I was given a wad of money and shown to a black Range Rover that Dave was driving. When we got in, he started to fire questions at me.

'Where do you live? Who do you play football for? Where do you work? What's your boss's name?'

He was building up a picture of my life.

'This is the story, Rob. I'm Dave, I was originally from Yorkshire but I moved down here for work and I work with you, we play football for the same side. Got it?'

I nodded.

'And don't worry, mate. The place is crawling with armed cops. They'll be watching us all the way. In the unlikely event you get taken, just go with it, they won't get away.'

I gulped.

And almost as an afterthought: 'If they pull a gun, hit the deck.'

I hoped he was joking.

We parked up at the mall and made our way through the Monday morning shoppers. It was busy and I could see Dave mouthing words. I assumed he was miked up and talking to someone in a control room somewhere.

He led me into a Starbucks.

'Hang on here a minute, mate. I've just got to go and pick something up.'

He walked into the gents and came out a few seconds later. I have no idea what he was collecting. I didn't want to think.

When we got to Pizza Hut, I watched in awe as he scanned the room and gave an exact and precise assessment of everyone in it into his hidden mike. His mouth hardly moved.

I was carrying Paul's phone. It rang. The crook was on the other end of the line.

'Change of plan,' he said. 'Meet me in the top level outside Waterstones.'

We got in the lift and made our way to the rendezvous. The man waiting for us couldn't have looked more like a stereotypical crook. He was stocky with a broken nose, shaved head and tattoos on his neck. He looked rough.

As I walked up to him, he showed me a knife he was holding, hidden from view by a jacket over his arm.

'Don't try anything silly,' he hissed.

Dave was right by my side and positioned himself to react should anything happen.

I handed over the money and turned to leave. I wanted to get away as fast as I could. Dave whispered to me.

'Walk away quickly.'

We got in the lift and hurried to the car. Dave was talking into his hidden radio. There was a sense of urgency to his movements. He gunned the Range Rover and, as we pulled out of the car park, he put his foot down. I was pinned in the seat by the acceleration as he took a roundabout at speed and bombed round a corner.

'We're being followed,' he said coolly. I didn't know if he was talking to me or his radio. We sped down a dual carriageway and I looked in the wing mirror and saw a BMW struggling to keep up with us. At the next junction it turned off. Dave smiled.

'False alarm. Just a boy racer after a burn up,' he said.

I learned later that the con artist was arrested as soon as we'd left and that he pleaded guilty to a range of crimes including blackmail and was jailed for several years. They had so much evidence against him I didn't need to testify in court.

The day of the operation, I had to call in to work to explain why I wasn't going to be in.

Lee sighed when I spoke to him.

'It could only happen to you, Rob,' he said.

A few days later, Paul went back to Australia and life carried on as normal. We were both doing well, both on opposite sides of the globe. Some people would have been satisfied with that. Not me.

All my life my role models had struck out on their own, come up with ideas and doggedly pursued them. Mum and Dad had set up Rose Fashions from scratch and turned it into a profitable business. Dad was on the verge of going live with his website when the tsunami struck. Lee had built CV Library up from an idea everyone said would never work.

I'd been working at CV Library for over two years. Each year I went back to India for a holiday. I travelled and I also started visiting the home we first went to as children. It seemed a natural thing to do. I helped serve the food and helped in lessons with the teachers. I also played with the kids. Sometimes just spending time with them, playing football or cricket was more important to them than anything else. I felt an affinity with them, like we had some form of shared experience even though we were from very different backgrounds and places. In a way I suppose it may have made me feel closer to our parents. Mum, especially, had always done her best to instil in us a caring nature. She had always reminded us that we should help people less fortunate than ourselves and this philosophy was deeply ingrained in us. It ate away at me. I wanted something more than a career working for someone else. I didn't mind it at all, but I really wanted to be an entrepreneur and, on top of this, I also wanted to do something that would allow me to carry on my parents' legacy of giving. I didn't want to be a charity worker and I didn't want to start a charity, but I did want to do something in business that would enable me to help others, whether through donations or projects.

Increasingly I hung around in London. I enjoyed a decent social life. I went to festivals, I partied and, like most of the people my age I knew, I enjoyed a beer. Hangovers are a fact of life when you are in your early twenties and they were often accompanied by a certain phrase.

'I've got a mouth like Gandhi's flip flop!'

I heard it over and over again and it always made me smile. It also gave me an idea. Why had no one ever made a brand of flip flop called Gandhi's? Obviously there would be issues using the great Indian politician's name, but why not change the spelling? Gandys flip flops! Genius. What a great name for a brand. The association in the public consciousness between flip flops and the name Gandhi was already there thanks to the phrase. It was fun, it appealed to young people. It also fitted into our story, our travelling.

There wasn't a single Eureka moment when I came up with the concept. Every time I heard the phrase I thought about it. It started after a music festival in Clapham in south-west London and the name just stuck in my head.

I had no experience at all in the footwear industry but I felt an affinity with flip flops. When we travelled, if I wasn't barefoot I was wearing them. As a family, we spent years travelling like hippies and flip flops were the hippy footwear of choice; they were also the unofficial Forkan family uniform. It seemed to me there was a lot of synergy between the humble flip flop and my family story. There was the travelling, the fact we arrived back from Sri Lanka with bare feet, the poem 'Footprints in the Sand'. I also realized that a brand could be used to fund social projects in other parts of the world. First and foremost it would be about the products and the footwear, but profits from the sales could be used to help children in other parts of the world. I knew setting up a charity would be hard and would be a full-time job in itself; there are so many rules and regulations and fundraising is incredibly competitive. So, instead, I figured that I could set aside a percentage of the profits and give those funds to other charities that the brand would align with. Gandys would be a social enterprise. I looked at other companies that were doing similar things. The smoothie and juice firm Innocent had a very similar model. I decided to set aside 10 per cent of profits and use that to fund charitable enterprises.

I thought about it as a commercial proposition. I knew there was a market for flip flops. Everyone my age bought at least a pair a year and everyone wore them travelling. They had international appeal. There were already other manufacturers making them and one Brazilian brand, in particular, seemed to have a large corner of the market. Surely there was room for a competitor, for a cooler, younger brand? There needed to be a challenger. There wasn't necessarily a gap in the market, but I reckoned I could create one with the correct branding.

Once I'd made up my mind that it was a good idea, I started to research how to design and build my own brand. I never had any doubts that I could make it work. Like my father, I had the idea and I ran with it.

Initially I thought about creating a handmade product in a natural material. Something that looked authentic; something that you'd buy at a stall on your travels. No one else seemed to be making such a product. I could also imbue the values I'd learned into the brand. I could make it a social enterprise so it gave something back. I started to research the shoe business and initially I didn't mention it to Paul. I did tell a couple of friends. They laughed.

One weekend I called up a mate and asked if he wanted to come shopping in Croydon. When we got there, I went into every shop that sold shoes and bought all the flip flops I could. My mate thought I'd gone mad. I spent over £200 on them and I took them home and studied them to see how they were designed, what made them good, what made them bad. I looked at the materials used to see what was comfortable and what was durable. I wanted to know what made some flip flops good and others bad. I wanted to make a flip flop that would be better than all the others. I got fixated on it. I had to find out what worked, how the successful ones were getting into the market.

In the evenings I sat at a computer on Google researching details about footwear, flip flops, branding and marketing, rather than watching television. I sketched designs. That's where I came up with the idea of the Gandys prototype; the original rope and jute flip flop.

One morning over Skype I told Paul about what I'd been doing. In the back of my mind I always thought it would be good to have him on board, but I was going ahead with the plan anyway and he was having a good time and earning a decent salary in Australia. But he thought it was a cool idea.

I discovered a website where I could source a manufacturer. Alibaba.com is a veritable Aladdin's cave. It's a global online cash and carry where international manufacturers sell their wares in bulk. It's a China-based site and the owner is one of the richest men in China, where I've heard it has a bigger turnover than Amazon, PayPal and Yahoo! put together. It has every product in the world; anything you can think of, from tables and chairs to tractors and canoes. They're all available direct from the factory at wholesale prices. It is the epitome of today's global marketplace; whatever you want from wherever you want. And it had plenty of shoe manufacturers.

I started to email them to see which ones could make the kind of flip flop I had in mind. I'd seen rope-woven belts and thought that design would look good as the thong on a flip flop. I started drawing designs and found someone who was making jute bags in Mumbai, India. They told me they could take my design and make me a shoe.

At the time I already had a trip booked to India for a holiday so, while I was there, I visited the factory. It was very important to me to make sure I was happy with where the shoes were going to be made. I asked myself: Would I be proud of them? Would I wear them myself? Would I be happy putting them on a shelf for other people to buy and wear? I needed to tick those boxes in order to be satisfied. I also started to consider how I might be able to make the product work for others less fortunate than myself. I wanted to carry on the work my parents had started in India. I wanted to help children and orphans. In terms of manufacture, I also wanted to find somewhere to make the flip flops with decent working conditions.

The supplier in Mumbai seemed perfect. They assured me they could make my design and I got the first prototype made and sent to me in June 2011. I was immensely proud. The shoe had the Gandys logo stitched into the strap. I started to tell more people I knew about what I was doing. It was ad hoc market research. I wanted opinions from friends and people whose advice I valued. I'd kept Paul up to date with my progress too and he was supportive and excited about the progress I'd made. Other friends, however, were less than complimentary. Several laughed at the idea and told me it was stupid. In honesty, it all hurt. I could take criticism, but in some cases people dismissed the idea flatly and even mocked it. But I was unperturbed. I knew when Lee came up with the idea for CV Library, people dismissed it and told him it would never work. Several years later, he had turned it into a multi-million-pound business.

With role models such as Dad and Lee, I saw that anything was possible with hard work and determination. Making flip flops was not rocket science, after all, and I had faith that there was a market for what I was creating because, personally, I would have bought a pair of Gandys and I was aiming to sell to people like me and Paul.

I began negotiating with the supplier and fine-tuning the design. I made another trip to India, which coincided with Paul's twenty-first birthday. Being a guy, I'd typically forgotten the date and booked the trip without realizing. When Marie reminded me, I hatched a plan to surprise him. I booked a ticket from Mumbai to Melbourne, where he was living. The morning before his birthday I was in India and I Skyped him.

'What you up to?' I asked casually.

'Just getting ready for the party,' he explained.

'What party, what's the occasion?' I asked, faux-innocently.

'It's my birthday, Rob, it's my twenty-first!'

He was sharing a house with a friend of ours, Angus, from the UK.

'Mate! I'm so sorry, I completely forgot,' I feigned guilt. 'I've been so busy with the Gandys project it completely slipped my mind.'

'It just would have been nice to have had someone from the family here,' he sighed.

'Never mind, mate, you'll have a blast. Have a great time, eh?' I offered.

When I hung up, I went straight to the airport and boarded the eight-hour flight to Australia.

When I turned up to surprise my brother, I walked through the back door of his house late that afternoon, just as the party was getting started. I will never forget the look on his face. It was priceless. His jaw dropped and he went as white as a ghost. He genuinely couldn't believe it, he couldn't get his head around it. Just hours before, he'd been talking to me and I was in India. My brother is rarely speechless, but on that occasion he really didn't know what to say. He just stood there in complete shock.

Eventually he came round.

'Do you want a beer?' he offered.

I grabbed a cold one from him.

'Happy birthday, mate!' I laughed.

We had a good night. After drinks at his house, a group of us went out and the party continued into the early hours.

The following day I explained to Paul where I was up to with Gandys.

'The shoes look good. I visited the factory, I've negotiated a price, I'm ready to get a shipment over to the UK. I'm going to set a percentage of the profits aside and fund projects for children in India.'

I also had a long-term charitable strategy.

'Ultimately, I want to open a home in Mum and Dad's honour,' I explained.

Paul nodded.

'Where are you going to sell them?' he asked.

'Online. I'm going to get a website built.'

That was the initial plan. Gandys would be an online business. I'd go out and promote them with postcards and I'd use social media. I'd set up a Facebook page, I'd Tweet.

Paul listened intently.

'It'd be good to have you on board,' I offered. 'It'll be a massive brand. They look cool.'

I knew I was going to do it, I was one hundred per cent committed and had already spent money on the project. I wanted Paul to get involved, but it was his decision. I also had plans to get Mattie involved. He'd left school, had been to college and was becoming a talented designer. He had inherited Mum's artistic flair and had ambitions to be a graphic artist. He was also very much into his music. I helped him out and got him his first job with Lee at CV Library, where he did graphic design.

Paul was unsure at first. Why would he want to leave a good job and a decent salary in Australia to gamble on my idea? But the more I discussed possibilities with him, the more he could see the potential in what I was doing. He liked the concept and he liked the idea of doing something based around our travels and building a brand to give something back.

I was only with him in Australia for a couple of days before I had to head back to the UK. Before I went, I brought up the subject again.

'We could be partners, it'll be our brand,' I said.

He thought for a second. Then he smiled.

'OK, let's do it.'

Gandys became us, the Forkan brothers. I was pleased that Paul was on board. I knew his drive and determination would prove invaluable.

It took him about six months to come back. He had a lot of loose ends to wrap up in Australia as he'd been there for several years. He also wanted to see out the summer in the southern hemisphere and catch the start of the summer in the UK. It made sense to have him back as the weather got warmer as I reasoned that would be prime flip flop selling season.

I ordered the first batch of 500 pairs for summer 2011. I was still working for CV Library, but eventually handed my notice in and went to work with a mate in Guildford in his recruitment firm. I also moved there. Gandys was taking up more and more of my time and I didn't want to mess Lee around. The other job allowed me more flexibility to devote time to Gandys. Guildford was also a big town with a large student population, and I figured I'd be able to sell flip flops there.

By the time Paul arrived, the website had been built and Mattie had designed us a logo. It pulled together themes from our lives. We put a footprint in it to represent 'Footprints in the Sand' and taking a step in the right direction. We put a butterfly on it because Mum had stencilled them on the minibus we drove around in when we were kids. We also put a kingfisher in the logo as it was our dad's favourite beer while in India, and we felt that lots of bright colours showed our vibrant upbringing.

We had packaging and we were ready to go. We waited anxiously for the first shipment to arrive. Gandys was about to be launched.

CHAPTER 15

Teething Problems

WHEN THE FIRST shipment of jute shoes did arrive, my first reaction was disappointment that they weren't quite up to the standard that we had been hoping for. My heart sank when I opened the first package and pulled out a shoe. It didn't look like the polished, high-end product I had in mind. The sole under the jute was recycled rubber and looked cheap. The size was written in biro and looked to my novice eye to be wrong. I opened more and while the sole and the sizing concerned me, some appeared better than others. There and then I learned my first lesson about quality control. If you are building a brand you need to make sure that quality is consistent. I'd wanted my product to be handmade, but handmade meant inconsistency.

We loaded the shoes in the back of my car and stored them at my house. Then we started pumping them on social media.

The first-ever pair purchased were bought by someone in Germany.

I got a huge buzz when the order came through.

'We've got a global brand here!' I proclaimed to a bemused Paul.

The shoes retailed at £20 and, gradually, we started getting orders online. We'd watch the website inbox like hawks, waiting for the thrill of seeing an order come in. At the end of the day we'd package up the orders we had and Paul would run down to the post office to catch the last post. It was like an eBay business.

While I worked on the logistics, Paul became the sales team. He went out and about around Guildford, handing out postcards promoting the flip flops.

One night we went out together. It was student night in town and we wore our flip flops and T-shirts printed with 'I love Gandys'. We looked ridiculous; like a couple of hippies rather than entrepreneurs.

The drunk students we targeted laughed.

'What are you two idiots doing?' they asked. When we explained that we'd started a business and that a percentage of the profits were going to help fund projects in India, they laughed.

'Gandys flip flops! It's never going to work.'

We changed tack the following day and put postcards on windscreens in car parks, then ran home to see if we had orders by the end of the day. That was our logic.

We realized we couldn't just confine ourselves to Guildford and went further afield. We went to London and handed out postcards on Clapham Common. I took Rosie to Brighton beach and we sold pairs there.

Rosie has always been a huge supporter of Gandys. She grew up with Mum's musical genes and is a great singer and guitar player. While she was doing her GCSEs at school, she arranged a charity gig in the school hall for us to raise money to send over to India. She had a big circle of friends and even though Paul and I were engrossed in developing our business, we still managed to meet up now and then with our siblings.

Paul also began approaching retailers and we had varying degrees of success with small shops in Guildford. The first that agreed to stock our products was a place called Hemmingways. I still have a picture of our first flip flop on a shop shelf. There was no point-of-sale material to help it stand out. The single flip flop was sitting there next to a postcard about what we were doing, among loads of other brands.

While retailers were not totally dismissive, we were advised that we needed a few more colours.

At that point we didn't mention the tsunami or our story. We didn't put it out there because we didn't want it to look like we were using what had happened to us to garner any form of sympathy. It remained a subject that we didn't talk about to a large degree. Many of the friends we'd made since 2004 didn't even know we'd been orphaned. Through hard work and determination, we sold our shipment that first summer and although the original jute Gandys didn't prove too successful because of quality control issues (they broke when they got wet), we were told they definitely had potential. Since then, some of the biggest retailers have told us they liked them. Designer Paul Smith and retailer French Connection have professed an interest in them.

I genuinely loved that first batch, in spite of their flaws; they were comfortable and they were so cool. I'm proud they were the first ones we developed. They were just not that practical.

Probably the proudest thing about those early days was that we were able to send money to a children's home in Goa which paid for educational equipment. We'd made a difference. While we'd managed to sell our stock, I knew in order to grow we needed to relook at our product and so I started the development process again, this time looking at rubber products. I found a supplier in China and, through the winter, worked long and hard negotiating and designing until I had a product I was proud of. The manufacturer was also able to deliver much higher volumes that were of consistent quality. They also had capacity to fulfil orders quickly, so if we ran out or happened to win a big order, we could get products delivered as quickly as the five-week shipping time allowed. The quality of the product and packaging started to get better; it started to look like a proper brand. We were learning and taking steps in the right direction. We'd built up some momentum and needed to keep going, so we developed products quickly for the following spring. I was learning about logistics and cash flow. We needed to order ahead. Increasingly we realized that retailers were our best chance of winning big orders. When we had 500 pairs we could afford to sell them online, but we wanted to sell thousands not hundreds and in order to do that we needed to get them in shops as well as online. Shops ordered ahead and so we needed to have the stock available to fulfil orders. That meant paying for the product up front and then waiting to be paid by the retailer; the lag between us paying the manufacturer and the retailer paying us could be as long as nine months. We needed to market them properly and create a buzz by getting them featured in magazines and across other media. We also needed to stay true to our core values: that Gandys weren't just cool flip flops, they were a social enterprise too.

We moved. We knew there would be much more opportunity in London and so my friend from Fleet, Adam Burbridge, and I rented a flat in Brixton as he wanted to move to London too. Initially Paul rented a room in nearby Streatham, but after a while moved in with us as we realized it was pointless paying two lots of rent. We needed all the money we could get to keep the brand going. It was only a two-bedroom flat so Paul and I took it in turns to sleep on the sofa in the lounge. Adam was bemused by the whole situation. He was on board with what we were trying to achieve and supported us, but he also thought we were nuts. It couldn't have been an easy environment for him to live in. Gandys slowly took over the flat.

Paul and I continued to work in other jobs in the day. He worked in a paint shop, I worked in a software company based in Canary Wharf which I knew through CV Library. It was a stressful time. After work we'd both devote our nights to Gandys business.

Soon after he moved into the flat, Paul was driving in the New Forest in Hampshire on his way back from visiting friends and his car came off the road. He was travelling around 60 m.p.h. and hit a telephone pole. The force of the impact split the car. Amazingly, he walked away with just a few cuts and bruises. The police who attended the scene told him he was lucky to be alive. It was a statement we had heard many times before. Someone was watching over him that day and I think the experience galvanized his mind. He became even more committed to making Gandys a success and started spending every spare hour he had canvassing shops and outlets in the capital, trying to get them to stock our flip flops.

We had a piece of kit we were convinced would give us a competitive edge. The world had gone mad for iPads. Paul found a cheap second-hand one on Gumtree and bought it, hoping it would give him an air of cool when he went into the independent boutiques we planned to target.

And so our foray into the London fashion world began. We'd been on a steep learning curve. We started with an idea, developed a plan, equipped ourselves as best we could and never lost sight of our goal. We believed in what we were doing. We didn't doubt ourselves and we aimed high. We were not naive; we knew what we were up against because we had done our homework. If you go into major retailers such as Office or Sole Trader and look along the rows of shoes you see Nike, Converse (which is owned by Nike), Vans: all the big brands. Those shops don't readily give independents or young start-ups space on their shelves.

We decided on an area: Spitalfields Market in East London. It is a place renowned for cutting-edge fashion and full of young designers and independent boutiques. There would be no point trying to sell into major chains without a proven sales record. We wanted to establish our brand with select, elite fashion retailers first to give us more kudos when we began rolling out to wider markets.

We tried to think of gimmicks that would get us noticed. Paul made cupcakes in a friend's kitchen to give to buyers in the hope that they would charm them. He also tried to make a display stand which was, frankly, a bit rubbish.

The night before Paul's first serious sales foray, we sat down at the computer and designed a booklet which told the story of our brand. It explained who we were and included one sentence that explained we'd been caught up in the tsunami and that we were helping orphans.

Paul's dress sense can sometimes be best described as quirky and before he set off for the hip part of town he decided he needed to look the part and picked an outfit he hoped would mark him out as a young trendsetter. He wore a blazer, bright trousers, shoes, bright-coloured socks and a cravat. I thought he looked like an idiot. Bearing in mind our product wasn't cool at the time, his logic was that if he went out and looked cool, he would make the product look cool. And it worked. The first shop he approached placed an order. They assumed that if he looked like that and he had an iPad, the shoes must be all right.

While he was taking the details for the order, he was approached by a couple of girls who had been browsing in the shop. Obviously drawn by his outfit, they told him they were compiling a 'lookbook' for a magazine they worked for (a pictorial representation of what's deemed cool on the street) and asked if they could get a photo of him. He obliged and also handed them a few copies of the booklet we had produced the previous evening.

That first week Paul cold-called all across the capital with a bloody-minded determination. Some people laughed at him, others loved the brand and were hooked on the story behind the shoes. Wherever he went he handed out leaflets advertising Gandys flip flops. I joined him when I wasn't working. At the end of the week he'd secured a surprisingly decent amount of orders. We were over the moon.

Over a couple of beers in Gandys HQ on the Friday night, we took stock. We knew the product as it was then was not perfect and the website wasn't as good as it could have been, but still we were getting more positive overtures than negative. And, frankly, we ignored the negative. It wasn't in our nature to dwell on the bad stuff. We realized that if we could pull in that many orders with the business as it was – just one of us knocking on doors and a product that could be improved with more investment – we really had a decent chance of competing with the big boys if we could invest more.

The problem was cash flow. We were caught in the Catch 22 situation many smaller designers and manufacturers find themselves in. If a big order came in, we did not have the stock to fulfil it ourselves and had to alert the manufacturer in China which would then make the flip flops and ship them to us. We would pay for them but would have to wait to be paid by the retailer. We would need a lot of capital to fulfil a big order. We knew that if we were to move forward and expand, we needed to find investment.

I was turning this thought around in my head when, a couple of days later, I got an email which reiterated just how much potential Gandys had. The message was from Arcadia Group PLC, the UK's largest fashion retailer, which owns Topshop, Topman, Burton, Miss Selfridge and Wallis. It transpired that the two girls who had been so interested in Paul's quirky outfit had been working for the multinational company as trend-scouts and had reported back on our flip flops and the ethos behind them. The buyers at Arcadia liked what they heard and were interested in stocking our flip flops in one of their high street chains. They wanted to know about our pricing and our supplies.

It was a buzz reading that email and flattering to have interest from a household name. Some companies have to keep plugging away for years to build up the sort of interest that leads to commitments from major retailers. We had only been making flip flops for just over a year and already we had aroused the curiosity of one the country's biggest high-street brands who were offering a serious proposition, and if we had been out to make a quick buck we would have said yes. But Gandys was and is about much more than profit. To fund the orphanage I wanted to build we needed to make sure the brand had longevity. We needed to make our flip flops cool so they would sell and continue to sell year after year. The chain that Arcadia was offering us shelf space in was not the right fit for our vision. It wasn't young and funky enough.

We discussed it at length and thought long and hard. We knew the right thing to do for the type of business we wanted was to gracefully turn down the offer.

For a week we egged each other on.

'You do it,' I'd say to Paul, throwing him the phone.

'No, you,' he say, tossing it back. Neither of us had the bottle to call the buyer back and decline the offer. Instead, we just left it.

However, that interest did make me realize that Gandys had genuine potential and the following day I handed my notice in at work. I needed to commit all my time to the business and although it was a huge gamble because we still had to pay rent, I didn't hesitate. I walked away from my job hoping I was on the path to an exciting new adventure.

I joined Paul full time on the sales team, which consisted of the two of us. We divided the samples between us; Paul had the left feet, I had the right. We handed out fliers across town and we cold-called boutiques. We sent letters and emails to the heads of all the major retailers we wanted to see our flip flops stocked in.

Our front room in Brixton had become Gandys international HQ. It was ten foot by ten foot and filled with boxes of flip flops, business paraphernalia and marketing materials. We traded with China from a computer on the breakfast bar. The walls were decorated with Gandys point-of-sale posters and our 'Famous feet we want' chart, which was basically a clipboard of photos of the people we wanted to see wearing our brand. It included David Beckham, Kate Moss and all the usual style icon suspects. The kitchen table doubled as Paul's desk.

Our methods were about as unorthodox as you could get in the corporate world. We dropped in unannounced to try and secure appointments with some of the most important people in the country. One day we cold-called Philip Green, the head of Arcadia and one of the most influential businessmen in the world. We went to his offices with some flip flops and tried to get an appointment. While we had turned down one Arcadia retailer, we still wanted our products to be stocked in Topman.

We hatched a plot to get our flip flops featured in the upcoming 2012 London Olympics. We contacted Usain Bolt's management and asked if he would wear a pair of Gandys as he walked to the starting blocks of the 100 metre finals (we assumed he'd make the final). We called big investment companies. Most laughed at us. We were told we were too early-stage and that it would take years and years to prove ourselves in the tough retail environment before anyone serious would consider backing us with capital.

But we were making inroads. Joy, a chain of twenty stores in and around fashionable London districts, began stocking

Gandys. Others followed suit and within months we were in forty different stores and were struggling to finance the demand. We spent a lot of money on building the website, branding and packaging. The need for cash flow became even more urgent. We got a bigger order and we couldn't afford to pay for them.

We scraped the money together. Paul used some of his inheritance and we ordered thousands of pairs urgently. Unbeknown to us, the manufacturer we were using gave our products to a UK-based shipping agent we'd never used before. We waited anxiously for them to arrive on a container ship from China. We'd pick them up from Portsmouth in a rented van and deliver them ourselves to the retailer. We did everything ourselves.

However, when the shipment came to port and the agent notified us, we noticed that they had placed a huge premium on the order. We refused to pay it.

'That's our rate, pay it or you don't get the delivery,' we were told. And, to add to our problems, the company told us they would charge storage for every day the shoes sat in their warehouse.

We had never used the company before and hadn't agreed to the price. Our budgeting was so tight we couldn't afford to pay the extra. It seemed totally unfair. The guy we were dealing with was horrible. He wouldn't have any of it. We tried to appeal to his better nature and explained we were just starting out. We had £12,000 of product sitting in his warehouse and a retailer anxious to put it on their shelves. The shoes were being held to ransom.

It was an incredibly stressful time. While it was all going on I was out one evening in a club and the walls started to close in on me. I felt anxious, hot and stressed. It became worse and worse and eventually I was back in Sri Lanka, panicking and desperate to escape. I don't remember getting helped out of the venue and after, when my heart rate had stabilized, I was exhausted and slept for the best part of the following day. I hadn't had a flashback for a long time and the experience shook me.

Eventually we got in touch with another logistics company. A friend I knew worked there and he had a word with his boss about our situation. We struck a deal with the man and told him if he could help us out of the predicament we were in, we would use his firm for all future business.

He negotiated with the other company and told them in no uncertain terms that they were being unfair. In the end, we agreed terms. It still cost us way over the odds and we had to rely on help from others to get the cash together. We knew the money would be recouped because we had the Joy order. Angus, our friend from Australia, was one person who was willing to give us the money to clear the debt, and there were others who helped us too. We are still very grateful for that.

The delivery was released and Gandys flip flops found their first major retailer. It was a race against time to get them in the shops. The weather was warm and Joy wanted shoes on shelves. We hired a van and drove to collect the delivery, then spent two nights in the back of the van parked up outside the flat in Brixton barcoding each box to save time. Such nocturnal activity, added to the number of deliveries we were getting at the flat, meant that we were beginning to outstay our welcome in the rented flat. The neighbours were not impressed. We needed to find somewhere else to base ourselves.

It was a steep learning curve. We were skint and we knew we needed cash to keep going.

CHAPTER 16

How to Get Ahead in Business

GANDYS HAD TAKEN over our lives and our home. By that point in the project we had invested around £15,000 of our savings. We kept odd hours in the house: another reason why Adam was such a diamond. We were dealing more and more with our supplier in China and so we were running on eastern time, working into the early hours of the morning, chasing orders, emailing contacts and working on designs.

We continued to face inherent caution from big businesses who told us we were not established enough, that it would be a gamble to stock our products. We heard it time and time again and it often makes me question whether this default mode of extreme prudence is one of the reasons the economy was so slow to recover after the 2008 recession. Ambition is naturally stifled and it becomes very difficult for young start-ups to reach their full potential.

Thankfully we had both inherited our parents' indomitable spirit and, like me, Paul was imbued with a natural desire to learn and a fearlessness that had been hard-won in the aftermath of the tsunami. We both knew we were survivors and that, given determination and motivation, we could overcome hurdles. We shared a common vision and we wanted to do something that would honour our parents and fit with the ethos of giving they had engendered in us. We were both unfazed by anyone who doubted what we were doing.

Our efforts did not go unnoticed. A letter arrived from the legal department of one of our competitors informing us that part of one of our designs infringed their copyright. It was the first of several communications from the firm. We also took a call from their MD, who in fairness was a decent guy and even commended us on what we were trying to achieve.

Our reaction was twofold. In one sense, it was a very worrying, stressful time in our lives. However, in another sense, we could almost take it as a compliment that a major company saw us as serious players in the marketplace. We were being viewed as a viable commercial threat. We surmised that if the opposition didn't feel our product had legs, they would not be going to the trouble of contacting us.

The more we looked into the problem, the more complex it seemed to become. While no one owns the copyright on a particular product, you can own the rights to the design you use and the style you develop.

When we set out making our flip flops, we researched the market and looked at the other products being stocked in the retailers we wanted shelf space in. However, we had inadvertently got ourselves into a situation where there was an issue that we needed to address.

To start with, we thought that there must be a way around the problem. However, in the end we had to face up to it; while our products were branded differently and went under different names, there was a resemblance.

Changing our design would be costly at a time we could ill afford extra funds but we had no choice. In fact it looked so expensive on top of all the money we had already committed, we even had moments when we wondered whether we would have to give up on our dream. It was the most difficult problem our fledgling business had faced.

Finally we decided we couldn't let this be the end. We just had to go back to the drawing board. It cost us another painfully large sum to buy new moulds to use in the manufacturing process. We settled on a rope design that was more in keeping with the very first jute shoes we'd produced. However, these ones were made of rubber, so thankfully they would be more consistent in quality.

I don't begrudge the firm what they did. Over the years they had spent a lot of money developing their brand and they were perfectly entitled to protect it. And ultimately the episode motivated us. We didn't want to cause any trouble or upset people. We just wanted to prove that we could build a successful social enterprise, and that we could do it our way. But we did now realize that we needed more investment. We were never going to reach the level we wanted with the financial set-up we had. We were working hand to mouth, using the money from one order to fund the next. On paper we were making money, but because of the staggered cash flow we never seemed to have anything to invest. We needed more money but the big investment companies we approached laughed at us.

Things were reaching a make or break point and one evening Paul and I sat in the flat and had a discussion.

'I don't know how we are going to pay the rent next month,' I told him frankly.

He rubbed his cheek thoughtfully.

'How much do you reckon we'll need to manage the orders we have and to let us expand?' he asked.

I'd looked at the kind of companies who were at the level we aspired to be at, such as the shoe brand TOMS, and the smoothie maker, Innocent. They were people-driven, ethical businesses with an underlying ethos similar to ours. Each of them had invested between £200,000 and £300,000 to get going and to get their brands, products and websites right. In order to get our product right and to fulfil the orders we were getting an indication we were going to get, I calculated we would need a similar level of investment.

'I've got an idea,' I told Paul. 'Brothers' Den!'

He raised a quizzical eyebrow and beckoned for me to continue.

'Like Dragons' Den, but in reverse,' I explained.

The plan was this: we would invite investors to come and meet us, we would tell them about our story and our business and invite them to pitch to us and tell us why we should accept their offers of investment. We would carefully research and target people who shared a similar vision to ours. Half the problem we were encountering was getting noticed; I believed the Brother's Den idea was off-the-wall enough to grab attention. Paul agreed.

There was a pub just down the road from where we lived called

Grand Union. It had a beer garden out the back and in the garden there were raised beach cabins. It was an ideal location to hold the Brothers' Den sessions.

I spent a month researching the calibre of people I thought would be the right fit for our business. I read press cuttings, found contacts on LinkedIn, searched for seed investors, targeted people in the media and looked for people who had spoken out about social entrepreneurialism. I also found out who had been on the programme *Secret Millionaire*, a television programme where millionaire benefactors go undercover in deprived areas to investigate who needs their help.

I drew up a shortlist of one hundred people. They included IT developers, company directors, retail bosses and celebrities. I drafted an email that I hoped would get their attention. The email explained who we were, what we made, what our goal was, what we'd done in terms of orders and turnover and what our projections were. It detailed the major fashion retailers we had been in talks with and the forty boutiques we were already stocked in. It also gave very brief details about our lives and how we became orphans and how we were using our profits to fund a children's home in India. It included an invite: 'If you are interested, if you want to help us and be part of what we are doing, come and say hello.'

We got a great response. In business, if you want to get a reaction you have to do something creative. There are so many voices wanting to be heard in the corporate world and if you want to attract attention, you need to shout louder than the others. Brothers' Den did what I'd hoped and although the majority of the replies were a politely phrased no with encouraging sentiments, we received seven definite expressions of interest, each of which we invited along to the Brixton beach huts.

Over the space of a week, Paul and I met the seven prospective investors. It was summer 2012 and we wore our flip flops. Inside the cabin we lined up some samples and some of our point-of-sale displays. We didn't ask for a specific sum of money from any of the candidates; rather we asked them what, in their opinion, the business would need in order to progress. Out of the seven people we saw, three offered substantial investments, any of which would have made a huge difference to us.

It was overwhelming to be offered the chance to take Gandys on to the next level and so we decided not to rush into a decision. It wasn't about who could offer the most in terms of cash, it was about who could help us grow the business. We decided that of the three potentials, it could be advantageous to put two of them together, in much the same way that investors on Dragons' Den often join together to fund a business. We surmised that two people with different skills could work well and perhaps add more than just a single investor.

We invited them both along to a hotel in Surrey to meet each other and to discuss a possible collaboration. We were hoping for a convivial business meeting. What we'd perhaps failed to take into account was the fact that as successful, independent businessmen, they were both alpha males with a certain degree of commercial ego. They started arguing about their respective businesses and their differing ideas about what form the investment in Gandys should take. They were approaching the issue from the standpoint of competitors, rather than partners, and there was a large amount of posturing going on. They were supposed to be grilling us, but Paul and I ended up sitting there watching the fireworks. Looking back now, it was comical but at the time it was slightly uncomfortable. After an awkward hour in which the discussion often threatened to boil over into argument, they agreed to take a rain check and we told them we would be in touch with a decision.

Later that night one of the guys from the hotel meeting rang us. His name was Dominic List and we had immediately liked him when we met him at Grand Union. Dominic was one of the candidates I had found by researching people who had appeared on *Secret Millionaire*. Dominic had a solid track record of taking on small enterprises and quickly turning them into multi-million-pound-turnover businesses. While his mercantile credentials spoke for themselves, he also shared a similar mindset when it came to giving something back. He was a keen philanthropist and supported a number of charities, many of which focused on encouraging and enabling young people to concentrate their energies on developing the confidence and skills to succeed in life.

Dominic spoke to me on the phone.

'Don't make any decisions yet,' he said. 'Don't sign with anyone, come to my house, come and meet me and my wife and have lunch.'

So the following day we did.

He explained that as soon as he met us and heard about what we were doing, he knew he wanted to go forward with us.

'You have all the ingredients, it just needs a bit of tweaking,' he said.

We learned more about the type of person he is. He told us how he lets his staff have days off to do charity work and that he has a love of travel. He had lived in Thailand and had done charity work there. His company, Comtact, gave discounts to charities and he also did work for charity for free. His values were the same as ours and the more we saw of him, the more we liked him. He got our vision of giving back and was happy with that whereas other prospective investors had voiced a preference for the more traditional charitable route where a business makes the money first and then donates. We had always vowed to put money into the orphanage we funded as we progressed.

Dominic invited us to his offices to meet his staff. He wanted us to be comfortable with him as a person and to have a relationship beyond that of a business colleague. It had been a hard decision to make; to give over a part of the business we had created to another person. Because to us, it wasn't just a business. From the first time I had the idea for Gandys flip flops, it had belonged to Paul and me. It really was our life. It was our tribute to our parents. We had done everything we could to make sure their spirit of adventure and giving would run through the brand's DNA much as it ran through our DNA and it was vital that whoever went into business with us understood and respected that. Dominic did. He knew what it meant to us and he knew what it needed to get to fulfil its potential.

He made a substantial offer to help grow the brand. It was a decent-sized investment, but still not as much as some people would ask to create a national brand. For that he got just over thirty-five per cent of our business. He didn't just give us a bag full of money; when the money was needed, he released it. Initially we only spent what we needed to. We leased and bought a van and had it signed with our logo. It is unmissable on the streets of London. We made the required changes to our design and we beefed up the website and started looking for staff and office space. And we were free from the cash-flow stranglehold that was stopping us fulfilling large orders. Dominic guided us, but he didn't question what we were doing. He offered advice and support.

I have no doubt at all that we could never have grown Gandys from a madcap idea based on a common phrase into a viable business if it wasn't for our unconventional upbringing and our parents. Our experiences, good and bad, had made us resilient. We weren't put off by having to work incredibly long hours to try to create a business we could be proud of, and was a result of being thrown into the real world so young. We are not naive: we did, and still do, make mistakes but we learn from them quickly and we rarely make the same mistake twice. Our parents always encouraged us to get involved in their businesses. When we were out in India, Dad would always be looking for export opportunities and I would help with the negotiations. I would sit in on his meetings with suppliers and would question him about processes. As children, our parents had encouraged us to be observant and instilled in us the gift of curiosity. We'd been taught determination and veracity and it was these qualities that transferred over into our business dealings and allowed us to take the knocks, to look for solutions and to move on regardless. For these reasons Gandys is as much about Mum and Dad as it is about us.

We were extremely fortunate to have found someone who shared our values and vision and could help us take the next step.

CHAPTER 17

Tsunami Kids

DOMINIC'S INPUT WAS invaluable in terms of helping us expand and fulfil the orders that were beginning to come in. Having available cash flow eased things and allowed us to look at the growing business in big-picture terms, rather than stressing about every small detail. Just having the van helped. We no longer had to hire lorries!

The brand was building momentum. We designed bigger and better marketing material. The stands our flip flops hung on in the shops that stocked them stood out on shop floors. They were no longer tucked away on shelves. We sent out details to fashion magazines and began to get mentioned in the fashion press. The contract with Joy led to more stockists coming on board. Our plan was working. Gandys flip flops were being seen in the right places by the right people.

Dominic gave us vital advice and became a good friend as well as a sounding board. With our business knowledge growing, we went out and won more business.

We expanded our range. We started with seven colours and added new ones and new designs. We became flip flop geeks. We learned all there was to know about flip flop manufacture and that helped us create products people wanted. Rather than plastic or ethylene vinyl acetate (EVA or foam rubber) we used rubber because it was softer and more comfortable. Our shoes were more cushioned than most on the market. Just because they were flip flops didn't mean they had to be uncomfortable. We played around with designs and looked at the ideal location to fix the thong to the sole to make our shoes fit better and stop them flapping, thereby making them more durable.

We learned that, in order to stay ahead of the competition, we needed to innovate and update. Each season we issued new collections.

After several months searching for the right location, we found new premises and finally moved out of the Brixton flat. We were sad to say goodbye. It had been where it all started for us and we both still have fond memories of it. The neighbours were most probably less sorry to see the backs of us, however.

We moved to a place in a converted school in Clapham that combined office space with living space much more practically than in Brixton; it had purpose-built areas for each. We took in a lodger to help cover the costs. We also took on staff, starting off with one and building up to several. Some mornings they would have to knock on the door to start work as one of us would be getting out the shower. It was a quick commute to the office!

It was a real challenge to find young people who would fit in with the Gandys ethos. We were especially lucky with one of the first people we hired. Dominic helped us set up an entrepreneurial competition at Plymouth University, where he had studied. Becky had to make a four-hour bus journey to the resulting interview. After a brief internship she asked her lecturers if she could finish her course by studying in the evenings while working for us. She is our longest-serving employee, and has been brilliant.

The first really big order came from online retailer USC. We'd been hassling the buyers there for weeks: knocking on the door, sending emails and phoning in the hope of securing a meeting at which we could pitch Gandys to them. We were pretty sure that once we got through the front door we'd be able to win an order on the strength of the product we had. Finally we wore them down and met with one of their senior people, a man named Ian. We went along in our flip flops, told him a little of our story and explained our products, our values and our vision.

'I like what you are trying to do here,' he told us. 'I'm going to give you a shot.'

We tried to stop our enthusiasm boiling over, hiding behind a façade of professionalism.

Ian reached for a calculator to start working out margins.

'I'll give you your first break and you'll remember this day because after this they will go like dominos,' he smiled. As a trial he ordered a large quantity of stock from us. In eighteen months we'd gone from handing out postcards on the street and rushing home to see if we made a sale on our website to a big retailer saying yes.

Ian was right. After that we knuckled down even harder and won contracts with some of the biggest retailers in the UK and some of the most high-end department stores. Topman stocked us, Office stocked us, Accessorize stocked us. In Selfridges we built our own stand and display, in House of Fraser on Oxford Street I built a Gandys garden with Astroturf from B&Q and we gave free pedicures to anyone who bought a pair. We entered into partnership with Liberty department store and designed a range exclusively for them. We came up with marketing gimmicks. We celebrated national flip flop day.

I went to China. Paul and I had meetings with retailers in New York and Los Angeles. We started to get closer to the dream of being able to open a children's home in India on the tenth anniversary of the tsunami.

One of the biggest buzzes we got was seeing people wearing our shoes. It still makes me feel proud now and plenty of people wear them.

The first time, I was in Brixton with Rosie. We were walking along Brixton High Street and two people walked past, each wearing a pair of paisley print Liberty Gandys. We'd designed them with the print running round the edge as well as on the upper sole so they would be recognizable. It worked. I nudged Rosie and we both stared. It was awesome.

A short while later, Paul saw someone on the London Underground wearing a pair. He commented on them and asked the man where he'd bought them. He told him he'd got them from Sole Trader and, when Paul asked what was so good about them, the guy said he'd bought them because they looked cool.

We've seen people wear them all over the place now. We saw someone in a pair at a tattoo convention a while ago where Paul was considering getting the Gandys logo tattooed on his foot. Thankfully he didn't. I got messages from mates travelling all over the world to tell me they'd seen people in them.

The bigger the brand became, the more people asked why we were doing what we were doing. They questioned our motives for running a social enterprise. They didn't get why we wanted to fund a home in India. We never actually shared all of our story with people as we saw it as something deeply personal. It wasn't something we felt comfortable talking about. But, increasingly, we found ourselves trying to explain why we wanted to give something back. Some people couldn't get their heads around the idea that we wanted to do something good for others.

As Gandys picked up momentum, we realized that we would have to explain our motives and decided to let people know some of our story so they would understand why we had the drive and the values to help children in need.

In typical unorthodox style we figured that if we were going to tell our story, we'd tell it to the biggest fish in the media pond and so we got on the Tube and headed to the headquarters of the *Sun* newspaper to find Mr Rupert Murdoch. The *News of the World* had just closed down after the phone-hacking scandal and we figured that the paper's parent company, News International, might like an inspiring good news story.

We took along a pair of flip flops to give to Rupert, should we see him. I've since learned that he very rarely visits his offices but, amazingly, he was there the day we turned up and walked past us as we tried to convince the security guards to let us see him.

In the end we didn't get to see him but we did get interviewed by someone at the *Sun*. We also called at the *Daily Mirror*, who eventually ran the story but only included a short few paragraphs about Gandys and instead concentrated on the drama of the tsunami. It was disappointing but we learned a valuable lesson about doing PR. Journalists will always want a dramatic angle.

That piece sparked massive interest and we've not stopped fielding calls from newspapers, magazines and TV stations since. Within months we were on the front page of the *Evening Standard*, we were in the *Daily Telegraph*, the *Daily Mail* and the *Metro*.

In interviews Paul, who is usually the loud one, had a habit of clamming up and letting me do all the talking. We did several TV interviews and were invited on *Lorraine* on ITV to talk about our story when the movie *The Impossible* was released. We went to see it and found it powerful but harrowing to sit through. It was a fairly accurate portrayal of the tsunami and not something I'd choose to sit through again. As we waited to go live on *Lorraine*, they showed a particularly dramatic trailer for the film, then cut straight to Paul and me. We were in shock and were then expected to talk about our experience.

It would be naive to say that all the attention didn't help get our message out there, but we certainly didn't chase it and we found it difficult and uncomfortable to continue talking about losing our parents. One of the reasons we have written this book is to finally put our version of events out there and hopefully satisfy curiosity once and for all.

The media profile we gained meant we started to get recognized. People from our travels began to get in touch. Ian the Irishman Dad adopted in Goa emailed to say hello. Another person who had seen us at Colombo airport dropped us a line to wish us well and explain that when she read the story in the *Metro* about what we were doing she cried because she had always wondered what happened to the four barefoot kids. We also heard from the surfer guy who had rescued Rosie from the tree in Weligama.

Then, in 2013, a guy got in contact with us out of the blue. He sent us an email from a Hotmail account. His name was Mike and he said he wanted to meet up with us. We got it all the time, all sorts of people came out the woodwork, so we politely answered and asked what he wanted.

'I know you,' he wrote back. 'I just want a few minutes of your time.'

We were intrigued and we tried to arrange a time to meet, but were so busy it never happened and eventually Mike went quiet.

We forgot about it until a few months later when we got an email from a PA at a big architectural company in London. She informed us that the CEO of the company wanted to meet us.

We asked who he was and she told us his name. It was Mike, the same man who had emailed from the Hotmail account earlier in the year.

We were suitably intrigued and said one of us would go. He stipulated that we both needed to go.

'Do you reckon it's a wind-up?' I said to Paul.

'Dunno, mate, let's go along and see.'

So, a week later, we found ourselves in a glass and steel building in the City, waiting in a beautifully designed reception for Mike. His smart-suited PA came and ushered us into his office.

Mike was around fifty, smart and seemed perfectly nice. He offered us a drink.

'Starbucks? Costa? My PA will get it for you,' he said. Initially we just stared and didn't answer because, on entering Mike's office, the first thing that caught the eye was a big piece of art on the wall above his desk. It was just one word painted in large black capital letters on a white background. It left us speechless. It was the strongest swear word you can imagine.

He could see us looking at it baffled.

After a few seconds I spoke.

'I bet you get asked this all the time, but what the hell is that about?' I said pointing at the canvas.

Mike told us the story.

'I was in an art gallery. It was a charity function and there was a fairly well-known artist in there. He was painting whatever he felt like with the intention of auctioning his work to raise money. At one point a load of guys walked in the door. They'd all had a bit to drink and were being loud. They started talking to the artist, asking him what he was doing and, in turn, he asked who they were. They told him they were a group of investment bankers. He painted the first word that came to mind.' He pointed to the work on the wall. 'I bought it because I thought it was funny.'

We laughed and took him up on his offer of a coffee.

With the ice broken, Mike continued.

'Artwork aside, boys, you're probably wondering why you are here?'

We nodded.

'Let me tell you my story,' he began.

Mike explained that eight years previously he was sitting at home with his wife and newborn baby on Boxing Day. He had a successful business, a decent life, money and a loving family. He'd just enjoyed a lovely Christmas. His wife was doing the vegetables in the kitchen for the Boxing Day dinner they were having that night and the TV was on in the background.

The news caught Mike's eye and hit him like a sledgehammer.

'BOOM!' He said. 'The tsunami! I couldn't believe what I was seeing. It was biblical. I'd never seen anything like it. The destruction was appalling and I knew it would be a moment in history that everyone would remember.'

Mike told us that he'd looked around at all the trappings of his comfortable life and felt the need to go out there and help.

'I couldn't pull myself away from the news. I wanted to do something. That night I spoke about it with my wife but we decided it was too dangerous. I had a newborn to look after.'

He continued to follow the news and, by chance, a few days later he received a fax at his office. It read: 'four English kids, just arrived back, need your help'. It was from a friend of my sister who had worked at his company.

Mike had also grown up in the area Marie lived in and felt it was his opportunity to give something back. He found out that we were coming home with no possessions and that Marie was in urgent need of basics such as bunk beds and clothes for us.

Mike started helping out with money.

When Marie needed money to pay for solicitors to adopt Mattie, Rosie and Paul and stop them being taken into care, he helped. He also helped towards the extension she had built.

Everything suddenly made sense. We always suspected there was someone helping us and wondered how Marie could provide for us. We knew someone was giving us money and it was him.

'I didn't want to meet you when you were growing up because I didn't want to intrude and I didn't know the situation you were in. I didn't want to swoop in and save the day like a hero and I've not asked to meet you now because I want thanks or glory,' he explained.

He said he'd often talked about us and wondered what happened to us.

'I called you the Tsunami Kids. I'd say to my wife, "I wonder what the Tsunami Kids are doing?"'

'I didn't know what would happen to you when you arrived back from Sri Lanka. Frankly, I saw the house you went back to and the situation you were in and, to be honest, I expected you to be a bit of a write-off. I was scared to check up.'

Then he saw our story in the *Metro* and read what we were doing and the projects we were funding in India and he was blown away by it. He was a wealthy man; he had flash cars, a thriving business, a nice home.

'But other than having my children, seeing how well you have done for yourselves and seeing what you are now doing for others has given me one of the best feelings I've ever had,' he said.

He wanted to meet us simply to say well done.

It turned out to be quite an emotional day and we kept in contact with Mike and will always be grateful to him for what he selflessly did for us when we needed a guardian angel. We've had dinner a couple of times since and, a year later, when we moved to bigger offices he kitted out our new office with stuff from his old one.

We sent him a picture back, a jokey version of the painting we'd seen on his wall. We signed it *The Tsunami Kids*.

As our story gained traction, others started to get in contact. We were asked to go into schools, colleges and universities to talk about Gandys and our journey. It was ironic given that neither Paul nor I had proper mainstream schooling.

We were offered money to talk to businessmen and, as the story spread, people also started getting in touch with Gandys, offering donations. In 2013, we set up a foundation which sits separately from the company. The Gandys Foundation: Orphans for Orphans is a registered charity and funded from donations and profits from the footwear company. Although it was not our original intention to set up a charity, Gandys footwear had grown so big, it was the best way to keep our charitable interests and business interests separate. The foundation funds projects through partnerships. Along with the Foundation's committee, we decide where the money goes and what it's spent on.

We continued to come up with weird and wonderful ideas to keep people talking about Gandys. We have both always admired Richard Branson for his entrepreneurial and adventurous spirit and I wanted to get the famous businessman on board with the Gandys message. When we set up the Gandys garden in House of Fraser, I invited some of the marketing team down from Richard's company, Virgin.

'Wouldn't it be cool to get Richard wearing a pair for International Flip Flop Day?' I mentioned.

International Flip Flop Day had been around for a while but had never really taken off. It was a day in the year when people were supposed to wear their flip flops to work and donate to charity; a bit like jeans for genes. We adopted the idea and made it our own. We used social networking to build up awareness of it and sent requests to Richard.

Word got back to him and he agreed. He was photographed wearing a red pair on Necker, the island that he owns near the Virgin Islands in the Caribbean. And he bought a pair for each of his staff. In return, we renamed the shoes Necker Red.

From then on, Richard stocked each guest room on his paradise island retreat with a pair of Necker Red Gandys. He asked us to send a consignment to his house and from there he arranged to courier them over to the island. He asked for 300. Unfortunately when we did the paperwork for the order one of us (we still haven't been able to agree on who!) added an extra zero on the quantity and 3,000 pairs arrived at Richard's private home in Oxford. We hastily arranged for the deluge of extra footwear to be collected and returned.

Our business relationship with Richard continued. A year later, we were invited out to Jamaica to give a talk at the business centre Richard runs there, the Branson Business Centre, a hub for entrepreneurs where they can work, learn and network. It was a great trip and, while we were there, we spoke to many young business people about our story. We also visited a home for underprivileged children supported by the Marley Foundation.

As business boomed, we continued to strive to make contact with some of the biggest names in retail. Our parents had always encouraged us to be inquisitive and to be fearless, qualities which had stood us in good stead throughout our lives. We thought nothing of hounding people for meetings. One of our heroes has always been the designer Paul Smith. He's an icon in British fashion and we'd repeatedly tried to get a meeting with him. After around a year of to-ing and fro-ing, we finally went to his offices in London.

We weren't disappointed. Dressed impeccably in a suit, he looked the epitome of British style. His office was stuffed with quirky objects people had sent him over the years; it was organized chaos. There were toys from the eighties, a jacket worn by Usain Bolt, a picture of Paul with Alexa Chung, a bicycle sent to him from China. It was an Aladdin's cave of cool stuff.

We met him on 5 May 2014, Mum's birthday. We spent an afternoon with him, chatting about business, fashion and design and looking at areas where we could collaborate. Neither of us had discussed it but when we left Paul said: 'Don't you think it's weird that of all the days, we've met Paul Smith on Mum's birthday?'

It wasn't deliberate. It was chance that we were all available on that specific day. Mum was massively into art, design and fashion and there we were, meeting with one of the world's most famous fashion designers on her birthday. It was almost like it had been organized for us! Maybe it was a bit of divine intervention.

We were never afraid to ask or to stick our necks out to raise brand awareness. We devised stunts. One year, during a particularly wet summer, we started a campaign for more sunshine and launched a tongue-in-cheek petition to lobby the government for more sun. We took the petition to Downing Street where we made a joke protest along with a couple of girls in bikinis who we found in a backpackers' hostel. We had a Tannoy and were chanting: 'What do we want? Sun! When do we want it? Now!'

Some of our proudest moments so far have been when we've been recognized as inspirational young businessmen. Each time we get nominated for an award or are asked to get involved in a public campaign, we take it as testament to the good job our parents did instilling good values in us.

We were asked to be young ambassadors for the Princess Diana Awards, which recognize inspiring young people. It was a huge honour as the Diana Award is the only charity that bears the name of the late Diana, Princess of Wales, and is a legacy to her belief that young people have the power to change the world for the better. Diana was also Mum's idol. I remember vividly how, like thousands of others, she mourned when Princess Di died. She was distraught and had so much respect for the woman. As part of the process of being made ambassadors, Paul and I were invited to 10 Downing Street where we met the Prime Minister, David Cameron. Of course we wore our flip flops and while we were there someone commented that possibly the last person to meet a British PM in Downing Street wearing flip flops would have been Gandhi himself.

We became involved in a National Enterprise Award for 20,000 school children who all got the opportunity to design a pair of Gandys. In February 2014, we moved to new offices near Wimbledon and London Mayor Boris Johnson came along for our grand opening.

Then, later in the year, we were invited to Buckingham Palace for the launch of a new initiative searching for young leaders across the Commonwealth. There we met Princes William and Harry.

We walked around Buckingham Palace in our flip flops and chatted to the future king. It was surreal. We met two other brothers who we have huge admiration and respect for as they also lost someone truly great, yet in adversity they have worked hard and served the Commonwealth.

Prince William took one look at our choice of footwear and laughed.

'Are you here to use the swimming pool?' he asked.

As we talked about our lives and work, he told us that he lost his mum when he was fifteen.

'But you have to try and find the silver lining,' he said. Which I suppose is what we were doing with Gandys.

It set us thinking whether we could become the first ever flip flop brand to gain the royal warrant.

It was overwhelming how far we'd come. We went from being two brothers in our bedroom with an idea to create something sustainable and to use fashion as a force for good, to being recognized by Her Majesty the Queen for our efforts. The speed at which it all happened was head-spinning. Gandys became our life. We lived and breathed it. Our social lives were put on hold while we concentrated everything on growing the business. It was like having a child. It needed our time, it needed to be fed and nurtured and we watched it grow into something amazing.

CHAPTER 18

Sri Lanka, 2013

L**ATE IN 2013** we were approached with an offer that we both had to think long and hard about. We were asked to go back to Sri Lanka, the country that took everything from us. We'd not been back since 2004 and had never considered it. There were so many harrowing memories there and we wanted to leave them where they were.

But the offer was hard to refuse. We were given the opportunity to go back and make a real difference to some of the other victims of the disaster. It was hard to turn down and because of the personal cost of our last visit to the country, it would be one of the toughest things we had ever done, but also had the potential to be one of the most rewarding.

We also realized that perhaps we owed it to the country to do what we could to help. On our travels we had visited many Buddhist sites; I had Buddha tattooed on my arm. I liked the idea of karma, that you get what you give. The people of Sri Lanka were victims of one of the most devastating natural disasters in history. But even then, straight after the tragedy, moments of generosity deeply touched us. Even after losing so much, locals went out of their way to help Westerners. It didn't matter what religion or ethnicity you were, they just wanted to help. They had given so much.

As I considered whether to go, I thought about the boy who had lost everything, including his mother, and who decided to help us. I never knew his name but he took me to the police station and the hospital. The selflessness and courage deserved our deep gratitude and we wanted to honour that boy's bravery and the kindness of everyone by trying to make a difference in the lives of others. For him and for all the other people who helped, we couldn't refuse to return.

We were asked to go back by Peter Simon, the inspiring founder of Monsoon and Accessorize. Peter was born in Sri Lanka and started his business from humble beginnings on a market stall in Portobello Market in London. He now supports projects around the world through his business and is a dedicated philanthropist. He is the kind of person we aspire to. We share each other's ethical values, so when he approached us about a collaboration between Accessorize and Gandys, we said yes and were honoured as it was the first collaboration Accessorize had done with another brand. Funded by a global distribution agreement, we agreed to provide an education for over a thousand children over the next three years.

Nine years ago, when we were travelling home from Sri Lanka, we didn't have any shoes on our feet. In November 2013, we returned not only with shoes on our feet, but with a flip-flop brand and a global partnership that will help many children have a brighter future.

Before we went we were too busy to think about the thoughts and feelings we would experience and didn't consider the impact it would have on us.

But on the flight Paul started to get that familiar uneasy feeling as we approached the island by air. And although we tried to hide our nerves and anxiety at first, it suddenly hit us as we started to hear the stories of some of the people who had tried to piece their lives back together after the wave struck.

Initially we stayed in Colombo. It felt good to be back in the organized chaos of a foreign city and with so much activity around us we were our usual chirpy selves. We both enjoyed racing around the hectic city in rickshaws and visiting some of the projects our Accessorize partnership would fund there. Paul and I laughed about the difference in rickshaw prices – for a one-mile journey one driver charged 500 rupees, while another charged 10,000. Some tourists would get angry about the obvious attempt to make a fast buck but, thanks to our travelling experiences, we realized that they were just trying to make a living.

At the first project we met some incredible kids and we were invited to take part in a lesson. Paul tried his hand at teaching chemistry but before long the teacher took over in case he blew the classroom up!

'I was never much good at school,' he shrugged as he was carefully ushered away from the Bunsen burner. Afterwards, we played some football with the kids but had to wave the white flag when the heat got the better of us.

In the late afternoon we met a young boy who had also been caught in the tsunami and had lost both his parents. He was just five years old when he was taken in by his relatives, but due to bad care he was later placed in a home. The locals explained our story to him and even though he'd lost everything, his face dropped when he heard about our experience and tears of empathy welled up in his eyes. We knew each other's pain only too well.

Then we found out that he had gone on to be abused. It was horrific to hear that the poor boy had survived the tsunami only to fall victim to more human tragedy. It highlighted for us why Gandys exists. The young boy particularly liked cricket so we bought him some new cricket gear and arranged to pay for cricket coaching for him as Paul and I both turned to sport for a distraction when we got back to the UK. It helped us cope and gave us a focus away from the grief.

The scars we both thought had healed seemed to open up after that. Neither of us slept on our first night. We were up all night watching the sea out the window of the hotel to make sure we'd be ready if anything happened. I found the sound and sight of the ocean unsettling. I listened for changes in the rhythm of the waves. I was back in 2004, on the building site that first night without Mum and Dad, watching and listening, plotting an escape route. As children we had been warned that Mother Nature was the most powerful thing there is and that night the lesson rang through my head.

The following day we were tired but perked up when we got the chance to meet David Cameron at Colombo Cricket Club, where we also met the best Test bowler of all time, Muttiah Muralitharan. The inspiring player has a great charitable project in the south near Weligama which, as a consequence, has a lot of young tsunami victims in its care. We had seen the PM in Downing Street a few months previously and he talked to us about the trip. He was over in Sri Lanka on government business and seemed genuinely interested in what we were doing. He was friendly and down-to-earth. I have respect for him. It can't be an easy job being the prime minister; I wouldn't want to do it.

Later we met another young man who had lost both parents in the tsunami. He'd gone on to be captain of the under-nineteen national cricket team and deserved huge credit for turning his life around.

While we had some great moments, we were constantly aware of being back in the country where our lives changed for ever. The memories constantly forced themselves to the front of our minds and it was difficult to hear the stories of survivors. We met a young boy who would have been close to Paul's age when the tsunami hit and who still bore the mental scars of what had happened to him. We both recognized the fear that was etched in his eyes almost nine years later.

Before we left, Typhoon Haiyan had torn a destructive path through the Philippines and we'd both watched the horrendous disaster unfold on the news. The realization that havoc was still a part of life in many tropical areas made us even more nervous and we started to get paranoid that something would happen while we were in Sri Lanka. Perhaps it was selfish, but it was almost impossible not to think about it. We couldn't sleep again on the second night and sat up talking. We both seriously considered calling it a day and returning home. But when we'd announced on social media that we were going on the trip we'd received so many messages of support and they convinced us that we needed to stay.

We continued and visited other projects with Peter. We learned a lot from him about retail, fashion and ethical trading. He was a great guy to be with and more than happy to get involved. At one point he started singing a rendition of 'Yellow Submarine' after some children asked him to.

We visited one project for girls who were victims of abuse. The stories were truly horrific. The youngsters had been exposed to situations no one should have to deal with. As part of the therapy offered to the girls, they were encouraged to design and make their own jewellery. It was explained that initially the pieces tended to be very dark, but as time passed the girls started to make brighter and brighter pieces, which showed that they were coming to terms with their situations. The girls used a lotus as their logo because the lotus plant begins to grow in muddy water but eventually emerges to become something beautiful. The logo represented hope.

While we were there, we were asked to tell our story to the girls. One asked for our advice on turning a negative into a positive.

'Belief and perseverance will take anyone to their dreams,' we explained.

One girl asked: 'Please can I have an education?'

It made us realize why we do what we do. The long hours and the constant challenges we have faced as we built Gandys from nothing are all worth it if it can grant young people their dreams and help them out of difficult situations.

It was an emotional and challenging journey, a metaphor for the lives we've led. It started so raw but at the end we wanted to stay longer. We even walked down to the beach on the last day and stood by the sea. We didn't go south to Weligama. I think that will always remain a place lost to us, no matter how much we continue our travels.

We thought the trip would help us to forget. It didn't. We now know that the scars will always be a part of us and represent the life we have lived.

We still have lots more hard work ahead of us. We look forward to the challenge. Our parents spent years teaching us the values that have helped us achieve what we have. They showed us how fortunate we are and taught us not to turn away from adversity; to help and do what we can so others may have the chances we have had. We were lucky. When we got back from Sri Lanka after the tsunami, we had people who helped. A lot of the kids we met when we went back didn't have that luxury and relied on the generosity of strangers. In future, Gandys will be able to provide help.

We started our mad flip-flop journey with the aim of opening our very own children's home in memory of our parents, which we initially hoped to do for the ten-year anniversary of the tsunami. That home is still a goal, and in 2014 we started looking for partners to work with the Foundation on that project. At the start it seemed like a massive challenge but, step by step, we are getting there. Being able to fund the project in Sri Lanka has given us a flavour of what can be achieved and we want to do bigger and better things. We've seen what is possible. We've defied the odds. We don't want 'thank you's; that's not why we do it. We were always looked after when we were brought up and even when tragedy struck, there were people who helped. We feel a duty to pass that on. We are in a position where we can help others and it's only right that we should.

I think, to some degree, the anger and annoyance I felt after the tsunami of not being able to do more for Mum and Dad has motivated me and subsequently inspired us both. Gandys helps us make sense of what happened. When we first returned from Sri Lanka, it felt like the tsunami had won. It seemed as if it had got the better of us, and Paul and I don't like losing; we play to win. As Gandys grows and spreads more good, it often feels that we're actually winning. Dad would always offer incentives to us to do better and to win. If we were playing cricket, the brother who scored the most runs would get a Mars Bar or extra pocket money. He taught us to be gracious, but to play to win and that is what drove us and continues to drive us. If we can create a super-brand and help people on the way, perhaps we'll have closure.

People often ask what our parents would have made of our progress. I don't think they would ever have anticipated we'd be doing what we are, but I hope they'd be immensely proud. I'm pretty sure they would be proud of all of us.

Rosie went to college, did her A Levels and set off on her own travels, aged nineteen. We designed her a pair of her own exclusive Gandys for the journey, decorated with roses. At the time of writing she was heading to New Zealand and then on to Australia and Asia and considering where life would lead her. She has expressed an interest in working for Gandys, but we're not going to put pressure on her. That will be her decision. Marie now has three lovely kids, Kieron, Isabel and Jack, and put her own life on hold to raise us. Mattie is a pure creative, sometimes in his own world but very talented, and Jo is making her way in the world.

In the months after the Sri Lankan trip I found myself thinking about the place more and more. There was an invisible link anchoring us to it, whether we liked it or not. We were now funding projects there and it felt good to be helping. But I had a feeling that would not be the end of our relationship with the country in which our fight for survival began.

Ten Years On

NO **ANNIVERSARY WAS** ever easy. Each year, as Boxing Day approached, we'd all be thinking about what the date meant for us and what we'd lost on the day the wave came. We all dealt with our feelings in different ways. As each December approached it was inevitable that thoughts would turn to the tsunami, and I was always apprehensive as the end of the year loomed. While we tried to do Christmas as normally as possible, I often just wanted it to pass quickly and was glad when it was over. Marie had her children and so had a focus and a reason to get in the festive mood but it must have been hard for her each year, on the one hand making Christmas special for her family but on the other having the reminder of what Boxing Day had taken from her. For Paul and me it was a day that had lost its festive meaning. We usually just wanted to get through to New Year, have a few drinks and get back to work.

As the years went on, the anniversaries did get easier, however. It's a cliché, but time healed. The raw wounds became scars. The sense of loss was always there but eventually we were able to look back and be thankful for having had parents like ours, rather than be bereft with sadness because we had lost them.

Gandys gave Paul and me a positive focus and we buried ourselves in the business. The two years running up to the tenth anniversary had been crazy. We'd barely stopped to consider all we'd achieved. We lived and breathed flip flops to the detriment of our family lives, our social lives and our love lives. Flip flops came first. Neither of us had time for anything else.

As the tenth anniversary drew nearer, I started to feel the weight of expectation looming over me. It was a bigger deal than the anniversaries that had gone before. There would be documentaries on television and commemorations around the world. I tried to put it to the back of my mind and continued working hard. I had no plans to mark the occasion in any special way. Of course the memories would be there but I didn't want to commit myself to doing anything specific because I had no idea how I would feel on the day.

As the year progressed we became busier and busier. In 2014 we sold around half a million flip flops and were stocked in over thirty countries. You could buy a pair of Gandys in Hong Kong, China, Amsterdam, Brazil, Singapore, Greece, Thailand, Germany, France, Spain and Dubai. We had started looking into expanding into the US, and had travelled there for meetings, but decided to hold off for strategic reasons. In all the other territories we had what were called supplied distribution deals, which meant that other companies – middle men – distributed the stock. We wanted to expand in the US in the same way we had launched in the UK, as the sole distributor. That remains an ambition and we hope to achieve it in the next year or so.

In the meantime, Gandys went global and we travelled all over the world for meetings. While business travel was very different to the sort of travelling Paul and I had enjoyed a few years previously, we were still able to appreciate the adventure of seeing new cities and we always took backpacks. We weren't your average business travellers.

The summer of 2014 was a whirl of meetings, festivals and expansion. It turned out to be a warm, sunny few months, which was great for business and much better than the wash-out we'd had a few years before. We took Gandys to several of the big festivals and hired a huge inflatable tent, printed with a map of the world. Our favourite was the Isle of Wight V Festival.

Behind the scenes we worked on refining our range. The Liberty print designs had been a huge success and sold out. They had won us the gong for best footwear at the WGSN Global Fashion Awards and later in the year we were approached to do another collaboration with another national retailer and an iconic brand. The Oasis chain was designing a range of clothes using heritage prints from the archives of the Victoria and Albert Museum and they asked Gandys to go into partnership with them to create a line of flip flops for summer 2015. To launch the project we were invited along to a star-studded party at the famous London museum, where we had the honour of seeing a pair of Gandys flip flops on display in a glass case. I'm not sure but I'm willing to bet they were the first flip flops ever to go on display in the Victoria and Albert Museum!

As the year went on and the tenth anniversary approached, we couldn't help but consider the underlying mission we had always set out to achieve. When we started Gandys we'd planned to use profits from the business to open a children's home in our parents' honour. And in a few short years we'd been able to make enough money through the Gandys Foundation to supply funds to a number of projects, including Mango Tree, a charity that helped disadvantaged children in Goa, and also the Sri Lankan schemes in partnership with Accessorize. But we still had the aim of setting up our own children's home.

As our story spread, several people and organizations got in touch with us to enquire about funding. We helped some of them, and as luck would have it, in early 2014 we were put in touch with a Sri Lankan lady who lived in the UK and raised funds for projects for children in her homeland. She told us about a small school in a village halfway between Colombo and Weligama that had run out of funds. It was a vital part of the community but was run-down and struggling. The more we spoke to her, the more we realized it was just the sort of project that we could help. What's more, the village was called Mau Gama, which means Mother's Village in native Sri Lankan. It seemed very fitting!

There were already capable people in the village who had experience of the area and its needs, and who would be able to work on the project for us. We started drawing up firm plans and investigating how we could help and what we could do. The plans grew and we proposed buying a plot of land to build a new centre for a school and community hub that the children and adults could use. There were hundreds of people in the village and the centre would benefit them all. We worked out a business plan; we didn't just want to hand over money, we wanted to create a legacy and build something that would be sustainable. We wanted the centre to be part self-funding so it could earn an income, expand its services and be hired out for functions. The land around it would be used to grow food for the community, local doctors would be able to use it, and in the evenings it could be turned over for community use and adult learning.

In the summer of 2014 the plans were well under way and we were finally committed to fulfilling our mission. We came up with a name: the project would be called Gandys Kids Campus. We hoped it would be the first of many.

Life was changing for both Paul and me. For several years, we'd had no time for relationships. We were married to Gandys. There was no room for anything else. But within a few months of each other we both found ourselves meeting girls. Neither of us were looking.

I met Errin at a work function. I'm not sure what she saw in me because at the time I couldn't have been grumpier (which is very out of character!) It was a Friday night and I was at a charity function in a cool shop called Aida in Shoreditch in London. No disrespect to the lovely people there but it had been a very long week and I was knackered. I just wanted to go home. Everyone else seemed to be enjoying themselves and enjoying the bar but I wasn't in the mood.

But then an attractive, petite girl who had been talking to one of my colleagues began chatting to me and suddenly I didn't want to go home any more. Errin was well travelled and her job as an events producer took her all over the world. We had a lot in common and conversation was easy and fun. Before I left we arranged to meet up and went on a few dates. On one of the first dates we had I sat on my phone dealing with a fire that had broken out on our premises and needed immediate attention. There wasn't anything else I could do about it and thankfully Errin understood. The relationship worked despite my apparent rudeness! We both had similar lifestyles and so we understood each other. It was good to have balance in my life. I'd been so focused on the business, I'd forgotten that there are other things in life that are just as important. Around the same time, Paul met a girl at a work function too and is very happy.

As summer came to an end we were increasingly being contacted and asked to do interviews and to give our thoughts and feelings on the tenth anniversary.

'What will you be doing? How will you mark it?' We didn't have an answer because at the time we didn't know, so I told people I'd be playing board games and eating chocolate like everyone else. I must have been asked a hundred times and in a strange way the renewed interest in the subject matter made the impending anniversary easier to face. In previous years we had all felt a little out of place and anxious in the run-up to Christmas and Boxing Day. While the rest of the nation was in the full throes of the preparations for the subsequent blowout, we would often be muted and introspective. But 2014 was different. Because there was a global conversation and awareness about the importance of the anniversary, we didn't feel as if we were on the periphery of everything else that was going on around us. People understood.

Meanwhile, as the year rolled on we hit the milestone of getting our one millionth 'like' on Facebook and also began talks with the designers at Pretty Green, Liam Gallagher's clothing range. We put in place plans for a collaboration with them and were told that Liam likes the Gandys brand and what we are trying to achieve, which was a big compliment.

Over in Sri Lanka things progressed quickly. At the beginning of November we finalized the deal to buy the land on which the campus would be built. We got constant updates on the progress of the build and were sent photographs every few days. Soon after the land was bought, a local Buddhist monk blessed the plot in a ceremony attended by a crowd of mothers and children from the village. We were sent pictures of the event. They were all dressed in bright clothing and smiling in the sun, standing on a large, empty patch of red earth. Some of the children were holding posters, on one the words 'Thank you, we love you' were written in large colourful letters. Soon after, a team of local tradesmen, many dressed in traditional sarongs, got to work. Within three weeks the transformation was incredible. The workforce had cleared the site, dug the foundations and started to build the two-storey structure. The local community were all behind the project and some pitched in to help. There was a buzz in the village around what was taking shape that we could feel even on the other side of the planet! We were getting just as excited in the UK. It really started to dawn on us that the dream we had been working towards was actually going to come true and we wanted to be there to see it happen.

I can't remember when we made the decision, but as work progressed Paul and I realized that the best place we could be on the tenth anniversary was back where it had all started, in Sri Lanka at the children's centre we were building in our parents' honour. It seemed right. We didn't want fanfare, we didn't want photographers and reporters as had been the case the previous year. It would be a personal journey. Marie, Jo, Rosie and Mattie gave their blessing and in the middle of December we boarded a plane at Heathrow Airport and, for the second time in just over a year, set off for the island in the Indian Ocean to which our lives seemed inextricably bound.

We landed in Colombo, where we stayed for a while before heading inland and down the coast to Mau Gama. The route we took would have been roughly the same as the journey in reverse that we had travelled a decade before, as we fled the devastation on the coast without our parents. Although it helped that we had returned to Sri Lanka since, it still felt weird being back. I think it will take several journeys before that feeling subsides. But our 2014 trip was full of joy. We were met at the village by a welcoming committee of children and adults. We were both amazed at the progress of the campus. It was bigger than we'd imagined. There was room for 400 pupils. The land around it had already been planted with crops and the completed part had been painted blue. There were colourful flags all around the building fluttering in the wind.

'Do you think they'll be able to put white stripes on it?' Paul whispered as we stood at the front of the building. I laughed. He was referring to the colours of our favourite football team, QPR.

'It's what dad would have wanted,' he smiled.

'I'm not sure that would be appropriate,' I giggled, 'but I get your point.'

We stayed near the village and over the following days we met the people who would be working with Gandys Foundation to run the campus. We met the children who would be using it. They were all from poor backgrounds and an education would give them the opportunity to break the cycle of poverty many of them were destined to be trapped in. We spent days helping out in classes. It reminded me of the work our parents had encouraged us to do in India.

One afternoon I started talking to one of the mothers who had children enlisted in classes at the campus. She asked me why we were helping and I explained our story to her. As I told her about losing my parents in the tsunami I could see her eyes fill with tears.

'I lost my parents too,' she told me.

She had also been orphaned by the wave and struggled to survive in the aftermath. She'd had children and was raising them without support. She thanked Gandys and all our supporters for setting up the campus and for giving her kids a chance. And she explained that she had enrolled for evening classes to improve her English. Her story encapsulated the spirit of the project and that night I went to sleep feeling satisfied that all the hard work of the previous years was paying off.

The next night the builders on the project took us out for a drink. It was a fun night in a remote bar in rural Sri Lanka. They were a great bunch of guys and persuaded us to try some of the local hooch, which we regretted the following morning!

It was a wonderful few days and truly inspiring to see the positivity and ambition of everyone involved. Although we'd planned to stay for the anniversary, the school broke up before Christmas and many of the families left to stay with relatives. The weather had also started to deteriorate dramatically. The winds picked up and the rain came lashing down. We felt it was time to move on and headed to a small resort on the coast halfway between Weligama and Colombo. Everywhere was quiet, much as it had been ten years previously. The weather continued to get worse. The winds reached typhoon force and Paul and I became spooked. We didn't want to get caught in the middle of another natural disaster. We stayed put on Christmas Day, had dinner on our own and, after a brief discussion, decided we had finished what we set out to achieve in Sri Lanka and that it was time to go home. We called the airline and changed our flights to the following day.

Early in the morning on Boxing Day 2014, Paul and I were doing what we'd done for much of our lives: we were travelling. We took a taxi up the coast. The villages and resorts that had been washed away had been rebuilt in the preceding years. While there were still scars if you scratched the surface, the resilience of the Sri Lankan people had triumphed over the physical devastation.

The motion of the journey felt comforting. We were both preoccupied with the requirements of travelling: packing, getting to the airport on time, checking flight times, making sure all our documents were in order. The momentum carried us through the day, away from one place and on to another. Away from the past and into the future. In the end the anniversary was an anti-climax. I liked it that way; we were distracted, we were moving, in motion, going between places. On the plane we had some time to reflect and stop to assess what we'd achieved and where we'd come from but not enough time to dwell.

When we got home we spent several days with Marie and the rest of the family. We spoke to Rosie, who was still having a whale of a time travelling. We had a belated Christmas lunch and let lanterns off and remembered our parents.

And then it was over and Paul and I got back to work knowing that if we get everything right we can get more and more homes built. We now plan to extend the Gandys range to make that happen, and expand into other shoes, bags, sunglasses and travel accessories.

We are still a couple of guys learning the ropes and making mistakes. We are not quite the finished article yet, there is still a lot of work to be done and we'll keep working hard to raise the bar and to open more Gandys Kids Campuses.

We had the most unorthodox of upbringings. We didn't go to school but we had two of the best teachers we could ever have wished for. While our peers were doing their GCSEs and playing in the park, we did something very different. We saw the world in all its beauty and also its horror. We are still doing something very different now.

There have been a lot of dark days on our journey. And there have been many people who inspired or helped us along the way. You can't do anything on your own, and we are deeply grateful for all the help we've been given. Without those people we wouldn't have been able to get through the dark days and achieve our goal of building our first children's home. We hope that more children's homes will follow, and we hope that sharing our story will help towards achieving that.

We know we can't help everyone, but we can help some people and if the chances we can provide lead them to set up their own companies or become doctors or engineers and help others then we've followed the example our parents set.

Children shouldn't have to worry about where the next meal will come from or where they are going to sleep at night. We had security, then we didn't and it was not nice. Now we are older and wiser we want to continue working hard to make sure that some kids don't have to face the kind of hardships we did or that at least when they do have the rug ripped from under them, someone is there helping. We've been through bad times but we got through them and so can others. Hopefully this story can give those caught in the maelstrom the hope that there is a silver lining, and that when the waters recede and you are left standing on your own in the debris there are people in the world who are willing to help.

ACKNOWLEDGEMENTS

To Marie, Jo, Mattie and Rosie and all the family and friends who have been there and supported us over the years: a huge and heartfelt thank you. Whether it's been support through the difficult times, a shoulder to cry on, a night out, a game of football or a weekend at a festival, we are and will always be grateful for everything you've done.

Lee and Brian at CV Library, thanks for the great memories. Dominic, Andriele and growing family: thank you for taking a gamble on two brothers with a crazy idea.

A big thank you to everyone who has helped out at Gandys and helped spread the word. You are too numerous to mention but you've given us the opportunity to create something special.

Thank you to Michael, Lesley, Hugh, Maddy and Gabby at Michael O'Mara for giving us the opportunity to tell our story.

A special thank you to Nick Harding who believed in this story from the start and whose expertise gave us a voice to tell it with.

Index